CW01276922

She who feels... knows

A Journey into self awareness

Maurisha Skyers

She who feels... knows

A Journey into self awareness

Maurisha Skyers

First publication October 2008
By Maurisha Skyers,
With the services of:
TamaRe House Publishers Ltd
www.tamarehouse.com
info@tamarehouse.com

Printed and Bound by Lightning Source, UK

ISBN: 978-1-906169-11-4

Registered with
The UK Copyright Service
No. 268566

Acknowledgements

I would like to say thank you
For everything you have done, and still continue to do
To everyone who has crossed my life path, even those of you
who don't have a clue.

"First of all..."
I give thanks to the Most High Creator,
For who I am and where I come from.
I would also like to thank my grandparents, my children,
My Step dad and, of course, my MUM!
To all the Seaforth and Skyers family,
For without you guys, I would never be.
Thanks to my biological dad for all my brothers and sisters,
Without you, none of us would have any existence.
To my adopted and extended family,
Who come with all my mum's friends,
That I have to call 'Aunty'.

To all my true friends who always have time for me,
No matter how, what, where or when it may be.
To all those that lent me money,
Without you guys, life would not be funny.
To all the true brothers,
Big shout out to all the baby mothers!
Especially you guys at the school;
Without you to pick up my kids
Life would definitely seem cruel

Secondly,
To those who educated me
Both on purpose and coincidently.
To all my school teachers and college tutors
Who provided me with that first, vital step
Toward my educated future.
Malcolm X, Martin Luther, Selassie... Bob Marley
Tupac, Luther Vandross, Janet Kay, Beanie and Bounty

1

Garnet Silk, Dennis Brown, Ja Cure and Sizzla Kalonji.

To my baby father -
You know who you are.
To all those who say: 'She thinks she's nice,'
And the confidence they gave me to write this book,
Thank you, I did not have to think twice.
To those in my community
For all they taught me all about:
How things are in reality, both the fun and laughter,
Negative minds: jealousy and insecurity.

Though everything that will be, will be,
You were all part of my destiny
Towards the day I learnt how to tune in to nature,
And realised my importance to the Creator.
Because of my lost identity, I did not have a clue
So once again, I just wanna say a big... **THANK YOU!**

Skye, Jayden and Rio
Keta & Colin Skyers
Abigail Melotte, C.J and Oneyka Skyers
Joy Cave, Lloyd Seaforth
Darwin, Garfield, Nigel
Dwayne, Zoe, Alisha, & Gavin Seaforth
Tomika Malcolm, Louise O'Connor, Leiona Townsend
Seth Washington, Debbie Wint
Yasmin Driver, Caily Marcus & Donald Wilson
Nicola Planter, Janet O'Connor,
Naomi Jules, Joan Bartley, Nicole Gordon
Lloyd Townsend Snr, Lloyd Townsend Jnr, Byron Parkes,
My younger Townsend Brothers and Sisters
(Dad made it impossible to fill the little space)
Sandra Nevers, Pauline Turnbull,
Swinda Mark, Daniel Blare,
Min Rebel, Paul Simons and OG Briggy
Redz, Andrew B, Mr C, Chino
Junior Banton, Mcgibbon
Iron, Fox, Marcus Brown
Charmaine, Shakira,
And to all who know me!

Dedication

Sonia, the angel sent to me by the Most High Father,
Disguised as one of my dad's other baby mothers.
I dedicate this book to you,
For all that you did for me when you were alive
And still spiritually continue to do.

"You always used to say"

"One foot is not enough fi walk."
And like your own, my "Mout' was specially mek fi talk"
'All what will be, will be
And will reflect throughout your destiny,
Maurisha, you just wait and see'.

The power of words is a gift
But it may also cause you problems,
Whoever you talk to, your words will tend to
Reach their inner parts and uplift or hurt them.
Many people are blind to what you see,
So they may often see you as crazy.
People may not like what you say
And prefer that you say it in another way.
But you keep going on and you keep being strong;
And Maurisha, don't let anyone ever tell you
That you're doing wrong.

"Sonia, it's only now that you're gone"

Its only now
I see why we always had a special connection.

Its only now
I see you were a reflection of my life's path direction.
African woman, so strong and wise,

Filled with the knowledge and overstanding
That has now opened *my* eyes.

I remember the very day, you told my dad,
"Cha! I can't be bothered to talk to you noh more,
God knows why he gave you daughters
And when Maurisha grows into a woman
She'll fix your b!?! c!?* business! And that's for sure!"
Now, I can clearly see that all those things you used to say
Have come to pass, or, coincidently, happened that way.

Sonia, now, I'm a 'big woman'
Your words of wisdom have been done.
The things I told my dad made him cry'
Just by making him have to face his own truths, deep inside.
Feeling somehow that you were there beside me,
Even though you had physically died.

"Now, through open eyes"

I don't believe in coincidence.
I know through Divine balance.
I know that in essence you were there,
And, that spiritually, you are everywhere.
You knew what will be, will be,
Just as the spirit now knows inside of me.

I know that you're physically gone
And your soul was called to move on,
Because your work in this physical realm was done
After many years of being physically, mentally
And spiritually strong.

Even though you only spent 41 on the Earth
Before you were taken away,
Your spirit divinely lives, and continues
In many people, each and every day.

Sonia,
I pray that as you look down
On what you have done for the All
You will be pleased, and
Sonia Ann Marie Malcolm, you can, **'Rest In Peace'**.

Contents

Introduction – 'Why?'

At twenty-seven years old I'd had enough of life. On the one hand I had three, beautiful children, the car I had always wished for, and the man of my dreams. I was living in a flat that was furnished to my liking and had a decent job. Yet on the other hand I was sick of life!

I was tired of getting up every morning and going to work.

I was tired of arguing with my man, and I was tired of shouting at my children.

I was tired of my financial responsibilities.

I was tired of a low income.

I was tired of car issues.

I was tired of my baby father, and his lack of taking responsibility.

I was tired of living in a cramped council flat.

I was tired of the housing benefit agency and the eternal cycle of their making mistakes and then claiming I owed them thousands of pounds.

I was tired of the gas man, the BT man, and the cable man, who never turned up for appointments, causing me countless days off work and issues with my boss.

I was tired of the police constantly pulling me over for no apparent reason.

I was tired of people calling me a *black bitch*.

I was devastated at my friend of thirteen years, who stabbed me in the back, because she was desperate to have a man.

I was tired of my fans, who love to do nothing but to make up scandals and stories of everything I seemed to do.

I was so sick and tired, until I was sick and tired of *being* sick and tired; it drove me crazy. So crazy, I vowed to find out the real meaning of life and why God would create human beings and then allow things to happen to them the way that they do. I wanted to know why we have to wake up so early in the morning and struggle all day long, to live a hard life. Forever looking, watching, wanting, hoping, dreaming and praying that one day we will find the perfect home, car, bank account and the partner that we have always hoped for. We go through hell and back to get and maintain them – only to find ourselves back in the same position. Only this time, it is with a new partner, a new car, older children with different needs and wants, and, a better job with more income, which equally amounts to larger outgoings.

Most of all, I wanted to know why this pattern reflected my race, *particularly*. I had not known one family member, associate, friend, or friend of a friend who had not experienced some kind of drama in their life. I did not know one 'Brother' who did not have two or more 'Baby mothers', plus two 'girls' and at least four kids. I wanted to know why our Black men feel the need to lie, cheat, abuse and neglect their woman and children the way they do. I wanted to know why our sisters put up with it. I wanted to know why, instead of supporting each other, black girls would spend hours on the phone spreading rumours, wanting to fight, or plotting to break up happy homes.

I was hurt, angry, confused and determined to get to the bottom of it. However, I did not know at that time that the search for knowledge and truth was part of my destiny. I did not realise that little bits of it had been falling into place ever since I was born, all the way up to the moment that I started writing this book, and it still continues.

"Life?"

I was never one to listen and always had to find out for myself. Through the grace of the down falls of life I experienced, I learnt each bitter lesson in the end. Finally I did not want to learn through the bitter lessons; I wanted to learn before it happened. It was then I started to research life by looking into Black history, ancient Egypt, British history, religions and the occult. I looked at various cultures and their traditions, astrology, physics, chemistry and biology; medicine, politics, and self. Through all this I managed to reveal many answers to the questions I had.

I can now recall many things that have been told to me by people throughout my life which now make sense, and, because I have become more aware, have great relevance to my life. Many of these people have said or done things to affect my life without their even knowing. There have also been those who knew and prayed that one day that I would too wake up.

'RIP Sonia Malcolm'.

I now see that every incident, coincidence or situation in my life was meant for a reason or planned as such. *"Yes mum! Even those rebellious teenage years!"*

Of course, we can go right off the good path, but from the lessons we receive in experiencing the wrong paths, we can always find our way back. On account of our disorientation, our eyes have been made to focus outwards, so we rarely look inward for truth. We prefer to remain in a circle of negativity, which equals a life of hell, and a world full of lost people. We constantly look for excuses, and to others, for reasons to explain our own downfalls or, to make us feel good about ourselves. We look outwards for the answers which actually lie within us, not knowing that issues of the self go far beyond issues of childhood, the past and wrong choices. They relate instead more fully to the issue of being, of personhood.

11

Interpretations of life have been twisted, turned and passed down to us in a form of Chinese whispers over the millions of years the Earth has factually been in existence. From this the term pre*his*toric arises. History is the story of 'others' and in particular, other *males*. What was before **his** story? and where are *her*stories?, What of 'Mother Africa'? What of *our*stories? Why are **my** stories a *mystery*?

Life is an experience with hidden lessons within it for you to learn about you. You can learn the purpose for your being, where you come from and where you are going. You have the choice to do whatever you want. However, we are all here for a reason and as long as you fight or ignore that reason, it will confront you and force you see it, one way or another.

Part 1

My Story

"I am a reflection of everything
And everything is a reflection of me...
I choose to see what I want to see,
I choose to be what I want to be."

1 Back in the days

I was born on Wednesday, the sixth of July, 1977, as Maurisha Amanda Seaforth.

I was fortunate enough to have a good childhood. I have no complaints. Mum worked hard every day of the week and always provided me with what I both needed and wanted. My Dad, like most of the black men at that period of time, had 'far more important' things do. But, conveniently, he found time to give me twenty-two other brothers and sisters. Fortunately, I had three uncles, who each lived with me and my mum at some point. So I effectively had three dads. I was the first born! I was everybody's 'Mishy, Mishy', and adored by all. When I was five my mum entered a new relationship. By the time I was eight, the two got married and mum was expecting a baby. I am proud to say that my mother and step father are still together today and have two children of their own.

At the age of eleven I started to develop my own mind, as opposed to doing what my mum told me I should, or should not, do. By this time I had gained knowledge from my parents and family, children on my local estate, and the elder boys and girls who attended the school holiday play centres in Peckham Rye adventure playground, Max roach log cabin, and Moonshot (community centre); so gathered that I had enough knowledge and street potential to start making decisions for myself.

By the first year of Westwood High School for girls, I had established around me a group of friends. Of course, in those days, it was called a *crew* as opposed to the *gang* of today.

My friends became more important to me than my family and home life. What my friends were doing became what I wanted to do.

Although I already learnt how to smoke cigarettes during my time at Max Roach play centre, it was here I began to smoke weed, or should I say 'Ash, Rocky and Black seal'. I stayed out till late hours and, on a few occasions, I would not come home for a few days. Although, if asked, my mum would say I ran away, I don't see it that way myself. It happened on an occasion that I was late home for more than five hours. I was just shit scared, despite the fact that I never got a beating in my life. I would always plan to get home on time, but somehow I'd always be late. I could not stand being the one who was not allowed to do what everyone else was doing. Not knowing that they too weren't allowed either, and half the time they ended up in just as much trouble as I did.

As for school, I was always a bright child, but my MOUTH stood in my way. I just could not manage to stop taking throughout the class. I always said, by way of excuse, that if the lesson were more interesting or actually had something to do with me, I would have paid more attention.

Guaranteed, every day I'd be late, both to and from school, despite the fact that I would leave both destinations well in time. In the mornings I'd hang around the bus stop, smoking as many fags as possible before registration. We would do this despite the fact that it was compulsory to attend morning assembly worship every day, *before* registration. After spraying half a can of *Impulse*™ liberally over our bodies and chewing our way through packets of gum, we devised a way of slipping into the crowds of pupils dispersing from the school hall. This was until one day our head of year decided to confront us by asking us about the topics discussed during the assembly. This was the day our well-crafted plans came unstuck, and morning worship became an essential part of my education!

Break times were my favourite. These were the times that I made money to replace the dinner money I had been given, but had used, for the cigarettes I had bought before school. I was an entrepreneur! I would sell just enough cigarettes, priced at 20p each, to buy lunch and still have enough to smoke for myself later.

I will never forget the morning that, whilst sitting at the back of the bus, as I did, I reached into my bag. My God! My cigarettes were gone! The box was there but instead of cigarettes there was a *note* from my mum and dad. "Dear Maurisha, if you were so ill, that you needed to ask us to write you a sick note to be excused from PE, then you won't be needing these. Neither will you need the sick note we wrote." My God! No dinner money, no 'fags'!, and I had to do PE.

As far as I was concerned I was not really doing anything wrong, my mum just did not understand me or how important it was for me to be there to impress, and fit in, with my friends. She did not understand that on many occasions I just happened to be in the wrong place at the wrong time. She did not understand that I had to be the one who was prepared to go where no one else would go. I was MAURISHA, strong headed and an independent thinker! I would know that what I was doing was not right, but I just could not help it. I had to see for myself, I did not want to hear, I wanted to feel.

After receiving countless letters from the school, having to call the police for fear I was hurt, groundings, confiscating my privileges, lectures and conversations about right and wrong, my mum was at the end of her tether.

By the age of fifteen and a half I finally got expelled from school for spraying CS Gas in the playground. I had obtained the small canister of gas from a male friend. We had met at the local bus stop at which both young men and women congregated in the mornings before school. Believe it or not I had actually taken it from him so that *he* would not get into trouble.

That was it! The expulsion was the last straw. My mum had had enough. Despite the fact that I had never bunked a day off school; that I had done reasonably well in all my classes, well enough to be entered for eight GCSEs, I still managed to mess it all up with one, ignorant and stupid mistake, and got thrown out of school three weeks before I was due to leave for college.

2 Becoming a woman

During the summer of 1993, once I had completed my exams at the centre for school drop outs, my mum decided to send me away for a long holiday to Miami, to stay with relatives. She gave me what she called, 'the last lecture', and suggested that I use the time to think about my life and the road of calamity to which it was leading. Being the caring and thoughtful mum that she is, she did not want me to go alone. So she arranged for my best friend, at the time, to go along with me.

Miami! Me and Yasmin! Did my mum love me or what?

I had been abroad before this, but this was different. The preparation for the trip was a blur. It was my first trip to America and the first trip that I had taken alone.

Whilst on holiday I hung around with my older cousins. To my surprise they were calmer and more mature and, they drove cars at 16! Wow! It was then that I decided I wanted to be grown up. The arrival of my sixteenth birthday the following week; the fact that I was finally leaving school and actually going to college; the break from my school friends and the development of my own dreams and wants helped me to decide that I was going to make a greater effort in my life. I was also definitely going to make sure that I would do whatever was necessary to learn to drive, and then to get a car.

I started college in September, 1993 and attended every single day. I concentrated on my work, with the intention of achieving a qualification in travel and eventually becoming employed as ground staff in either Heathrow or Gatwick airport. To my mother's delight, I stopped hanging around with old school friends. However, she did not know that it was not by choice but due to the fact that we lived in different areas and were, by now, attending different colleges.

All the hard work and effort I put in paid off. I passed my GNVQ with flying colours, gaining a distinction. I was quite chuffed. The following term I enrolled on a BTEC national diploma in business and finance.

It was then that I met my first, real, serious boyfriend, whom I started to spend most of my time with. He was a popular sound man from Peckham. He was cute, funny and loving but he came with a child. At the time I did not have a clue that for a man to have a *baby mother* was different to him having an ex girlfriend. She came round to his house, with the child, every day. On one occasion she pulled out a machete to attack me with, in the middle of Peckham, whilst expressing her feelings concerning my presence. She claimed that I was ruining her family and causing her pain. She told me that despite the fact that they were apart due to conflict over their personal issues, they still slept together. It was in this way I discovered my first lesson in 'baby mama drama'. Nevertheless I still continued the relationship because he would tell me that he loved me and that he really didn't want her and that she was using the child to trap him. I'd always fall for it. I was at his house almost every day, I became very close to his mother, his sister and his younger brother. They became my new family.

By the age of sixteen and a half I believed I was now a grown adult. So grown I seemed too old for the rules of my mother. I wanted to stay out late, go raving and sleep at my boyfriend's house. Of course neither my mum nor dad, were having any of it. So I was ready to move out, and do what *I* wanted to do, by any means necessary.

One week before my seventeenth birthday, I moved out and went into a hostel, and my boyfriend moved in with me. I lived my life to the fullest and enjoyed every moment.

Trust me that is a whole other book! But basically, I did what I wanted, when I wanted. There was not one *Lazerdrome, Champion Love, Live Wire, Fifth Avenue, Hyper Esq, Desi G and Barry White* rave put on that I did not go to. I controlled my life, and my freedom, or so I thought. Not actually realizing, when I was moving out, that I would also be in control of my discipline and the boundaries needing to be set, along with the financial aspects of 'living life'.

Driving lessons were definitely put on hold, and college was no longer fun without money to get there, or money for lunch. So, eventually, I gave it up.

Life was hard, but I soldiered on, as we do. I would pay my rent of four pounds, thanks to housing benefit. I would do a little food shopping and spend the rest of my money on *weed* and socializing, hoping for the best, not noticing that in some way, somehow, just in the nick of time, it would always come together. Through every set back, trial and tribulation, through every drink that my friends drank – from the one bottle of drink I had to last me till I received my next giro – I slowly began to experience, and so to understand, the things my mother used to say to me. Although one thing my mother never told me about, was love and broken hearts.

After my boyfriend's baby mother proudly poked her eight months pregnant belly in my face, one day at the prison gate. The calculations revealed that in fact she was telling the truth all along. It was right then and there I learnt my first experience of real pain. However, looking back now it wasn't so bad because this is where I experienced my first opportunity, to reflect on my worth, my wants and my needs and, eventually, made a decision to leave him.

It took some time and negotiation, but finally I got a flat, in one of the largest estates in the middle of Brixton. After a few months more of living life to the fullest, I got myself a full time job as a trainee hairdresser, earning a total income of forty-five pounds per week. I enjoyed the job and was doing well with my preparation for my NVQ level 1 hairdressing course, until one day I received an unexpected call. It was a call from a lady from the income support *fraud squad*. She told me that I had been illegally claiming money and that my benefits would be stopped. What this meant was that I was now going to be responsible for paying fifty nine pounds a week rent, council tax, gas and electricity *and* still manage to live, all on **forty-five pounds** per week. Well I never! I gave the job up straight away!, and spent the next few years out of work and living life! I knew that doing things this way I could make ends meet and my rent would still be paid!

3 Motherhood

At the age of nineteen, I became pregnant with my first child. She was born a beautiful and serene-natured baby girl. I named her Skye.

Unfortunately, my child was not fathered by someone with whom I was in a serious relationship, or, whom I felt a real, deep, all-consuming love for. He was just some guy I had been seeing for around five months. When I had the pregnancy test result for a short while I contemplated not telling him, to save me all the hardship I had seen most of the black women I knew go through. I figured that if I was going to have to do the whole child-rearing thing on my own, in the end, I might as well do it from the start. But, on the other hand, the excitement I felt just had to be shared; I could not keep this exciting news all to myself... I explained to him how I felt about the two of us becoming serious just because of having a child together, and then eventually ending up apart. He spun me a wheel of crap, as they do. I listened and accepted, as we do.

I decided to move out of the area. At nineteen years old I knew *Somerleyton Estate,* in the heart of Brixton, was not the place I wanted my child to grow up in. I did all I possibly could to get the local authority to move me.

During all this time he never did very much, apart from smile, and agree with everything I said. *"For real... for real..."* was his almost permanent expression. He never gave me money for the baby's stuff or made any contribution towards fixing up the new flat. Yet, I still continued on. The birth of my child was at the top of my priorities and although I could see he was no good, it had not really registered yet.

Some time before I had become pregnant I had gone to visit a girl friend of mine in prison and was caught passing her some cannabis. As a result of this I had a court case which had been pending for eight months. To my great surprise I was finally sentenced. Sentenced to twenty eight days imprisonment, six months into my pregnancy, despite the fact that the amount of cannabis was only valued at three pounds sixty eight pence. The judge implied that his decision was harsh, but I was to be used as an example. Even though I was not in the habit of doing such things and no longer hung around with this group of girls. Yet again I was forced to feel the wider reaction to my own, not well thought out, actions.

Although I saw myself as a 'bad gal', I must admit I did not feel comfortable around robbers, thieves, murderers or lesbians. I mean no offence to this last group, but we all have our preferences. By the end of week two I was ready to go home.

Funnily enough, when I think back on it, it was not too bad. The maternity wing came with special privileges, although these did not include skin cream, combs, phone cards or any of the other luxuries we take for granted on the outside. I did, however, get to relax and take time out, time to meditate, and really think about me. I went swimming and participated in pre-natal exercise classes offered. I was even allowed to watch *East Enders*.

My *babyfather* had accompanied me to court the day I received my sentence, so he had taken my belongings home and offered to keep an eye on my flat. What he did not tell me, though was that he was planning to move all his *shit* in whilst I was gone. And that he would be opening my letters and cashing my giros, with the intention of *chatting shit* by way of excusing himself when I confronted him later on. Despite the fact that the letter clearly stated: "*Please take this letter to the post office to collect your book. Enclosed is also a bank giro for one hundred and seventy pounds as back dated payment."* (Ladies, I'm sure you know the type of letter). And this was just the start!

Three months after my release from prison, my daughter was born, just before my twentieth birthday. On that day labour pain devoured my body. I did not feel like the same person anymore. I had now become a mother!

At first it took a little getting used to; waking up every day and putting someone else before me. I had to put my needs and wants on hold each day and make sacrifices. But thanks to the ten years prior experience of babysitting my little brother, sister, cousins, and my mum's friend's children I had gained some experience. Thanks to the nurturing spirit my mother had installed into me, I managed to adapt to motherhood just fine.

My baby father still did nothing much, apart from leech onto what I worked hard to achieve (and at times when I was not working), and play with the baby whilst I cooked dinner or cleaned the house. But somehow that one hundred and five pound income support would always manage to stretch to include gas and electricity bills, nappies, baby wipes, baby food, toiletries, food and clothes. It would also stretch to meet the *professional* baby photos, birthday gifts, Christmas presents and everything else that was needed in our home, or in our lives, at that time. Although I could clearly see that he was no good, I turned a blind eye, as Skye was the main focus of my life; my little bundle of joy.

My family would always tell me that she was the dead stamp of me, 'little mishy,' fass, nuff, a little miss chatter box. By nine months old she had begun to walk, by the age of three she was doing the latest dances from Jamaica and by the time she learned how to talk properly it has been impossible for me to get her to stop!

Exactly one year later, despite all the setbacks, I passed my driving test – and then found out day that I was pregnant again, with my sec turned out to be a boy child, Jayden.

I had always dreamt of having a son. Jayden was not like Skye, or me. He was, and is, still, very much like his dad. *'You have to keep a close eye on the quiet ones'*. Compared to Skye's ten hour labour, Jayden was a breeze, he was out half an hour after I arrived at the hospital!

Two children twenty months apart was hard, but Jayden was a very calm baby and very easy to please, besides, he had Skye to keep him company. He was not as talkative or as confident as Skye, but displayed his talents in his physicality.

From the age of three this child was breaking everything in sight with his football. He would wake up and go to sleep with a football, so, at the age of four I took him to the local Fulham club community session. At first he was shy and refused to take part, but after the third time of taking him there, as well as his dad threatening to throw away his football stuff if all he wanted to do with it was to destroy the house, he decided to take part. He was spotted instantly for his talent and I was invited to bring him along to the advanced training session for Fulham's under-six community team. Jayden trained for two years with the bigger boys until he was of age. He became the man of the match; every game, twisting, dodging and tackling boys twice his size; scoring goals like there was no tomorrow. Since then he has spent three evenings a week and all weekends playing football, until he finally got signed by Chelsea at the age of ten.

I was adamant that whatever it was going to take, my son was not going to be like every other black youth hanging around estates, selling drugs and sponging off women as his only means of succeeding in life. Having Skye around helped him to become one of the brightest in his class and being the dsome, happy lad he is, he was adored by all. It was rfect; I had my very own prince and princess.

However, the birth of this second child seemed to also be a stamp of authorization for my baby father, a confirmation of *'You can now take the piss, because I'm here to stay'.* He became physically and mentally abusive, demanding, and selfish and even more of a womanizer. He would drive my car and never put petrol in it; he would eat and drink the food but never buy it; he would use the gas, electricity and all the household appliances but never pay for them. He would hit me, kick me, spit on me, steal my money, steal every mobile phone I bought and trash my home. He sold my passport and TV out of my home. He would take my car and drive it until there was no more petrol, then leave it right where it stopped. He would crash my car, and leave me to fix it. Anytime I had anything to say, he would end up hitting me, or taking another of my possessions for all the 'trouble' I was giving him. Meanwhile **physically** I worked hard, getting up every day to go to work. **Mentally** I struggled; life was hell, full of constant worry, anxiety and stress. **Emotionally** I spent most of my time crying, being upset or angry at all I had to go through just to sustain a family, even feeling that I hated it all. **Spiritually** I felt very alone, isolated. Every time I decided to express my feelings it would always lead to an argument and I would always be left worse off, whilst he simply put his trainers on, and walked out the door.

Of course we never tell our family members the truth, so I spent a lot of time, over the years, phoning my friends, talking on the phone for hours about what I wanted to do and where I wanted to be. *'I have another bruise. I have had enough. He is taking the piss. I can't take this anymore. I'm going to go to a refuge. There is another girl...another baby'...* My friends listened to me babble on for years, some willing and understanding and some just out of loyalty for our friendship. I would leave many times, but for one reason or another, I would always go back; admittedly, most of the time I did not even want him. I just did not want to be alone. I just did not want to be another black single mum. Although I did not want him, I was now used to the family unit. But let's not escape the fact that all lot of time I actually felt sorry for this guy. He had no money, no ambition, no self respect and nowhere to live. So I held on to a life to a lifeless relationship, with someone whom, I had nothing in common with at all, from day one.

He was from a large family, which consisted mainly of women. I reached out to them many times for help. Funny, many of them would sit down and share stories of being a single mother and the hardship it brings; and on many occasions I saw them go through torture and torment. They would be so understanding at the time of our conversation, yet, after I was gone, my torture and torment became just another stripe on the 'mad baby mama drama' chart they had devised for me. This of course was not based on truth but firstly upon loyalty for their family member and secondly their extensions to his interpretations of the truth. To them it did not matter that a member of their family was not taking care of his responsibilities, it did not matter that a member of their family was abusing a woman, it did not matter that they themselves hid my car keys or purse for me anytime he entered my home. What I did and what I said became the focal point of every argument and family discussion. Finally I understood why he chose to address situations the way he did, and finally gave up looking to them for MORAL support.

Despite all of this, in September, 2001, at the age of twenty four, I had my third child, a boy, Rio. This pregnancy however, was very different. I had been told by medical staff at the hospital that my child was likely to be born disabled. Abnormalities were detected during a routine scan. The doctors told me that my baby's bowels were not being formed properly. They further added that if they were not working he could not release poisons and waste from his body and would eventually die. This bowel formation deficiency also led them to believe that he would also have physical defects.

As I was eighteen weeks pregnant, I was expected by the medical staff to abort the pregnancy and then give birth to a dead child. I was shown pictures of tiny coffins and offered a

27

follow-up counselling session. Well... I was devastated. However, although they told me something was wrong I did not feel any different compared to my other pregnancies and my heart would not have it any other way. I had already decided to keep my child regardless of any defects, but I had to know for sure.

Throughout a certain stage of my first pregnancy I had already begun to reach out to a higher purpose. I had started to attend local church meetings. They would give me Psalms to read which somehow would make me feel a ray of hope. I was especially drawn to the Psalm of David, which, coincidently, helped me through my fear of giving birth and also the anxiety of my driving test. However, this time I did not feel that the Bible was supplying all that I needed, so I went to see a psychic. She told me to have faith, and that my son would be fine. I will never forget her telling me, "*Your baby is fine...please tell the doctors, no, thank you, you know what God you serve.*" I so wanted it to be true, I believed it with all my heart and soul.

I returned to the hospital each week for monitoring scans. Each time the scan showed the same problem, and each week the nurse would stroke my shoulder with sympathy, but I never once let go of my faith.

During the scan scheduled one week before my expected due date, to the doctor's and nurse's surprise, the 'black hole' inside my son had totally disappeared. As I sat there and smiled, they sent for specialist after specialist.

Rio was my third child; a son. What can I say about him? Anyone who knows Rio will know that Rio is just Rio and there is no other like him in the whole universe. God knows he was a miracle. Rio is not and has never been simply a child. In his mind he is a grown man who knows exactly what, where and how he wants his life to be and he does not take no for an answer. At first I could not stay at anyone's house longer than one hour before wanting to go home. He would tear, rip and break everything in sight trying to discover what it could or could not do. If one thing was taken away from him, within a split second he already had gotten hold of something else. He liked to sleep on my head, lying across my face, tugging at my hair every night without fail. I cannot see why, but somehow he managed to find comfort in it.

Like Skye, Rio was advanced for his age, walking and talking long before his first birthday; this boy had no fear at all. I should have named him *Question*, because that's all he ever does, all day, every day. He even asked me once if he could have God's telephone number because he wanted to ask him a question. Now he's six and at school. One week I'll get a telephone call from the school about his 'poor' behaviour and then the next week he will come home and announce that he is elected as a school councillor. '*Mi dear*'!

Although I had always had faith in God, it was at that time I knew that God was actually real. This miracle of Rio's birth made me see life in a different way. I became more serious about my life. My kids were a main factor in this and I vowed to find a way out of the hellish relationship, and situation, I was in.

4 A strong black woman

Coincidently, the Christmas following Rio's birth, my cousin Daniel gave me a book written by Iyanla Vanzant called Faith in the Valley. It was inscribed: 'To Maurisha, a strong black woman'.

My cousin did not know at the time what, by that simple act, he was going to do to my life. In fact, I had always found it strange that, prior to that year, he had never given me a Christmas present, or, any kind of present come to think of it. I now call that gift an angel blessing. He was the angel.

I was never one to *really* read books; I owned several but never seemed to ever get past say, page twenty, without excuses of washing, cooking, cleaning, paying bills, dealing with kids and my baby father stress, although I *did* find time for reading gossip magazines. It was the inscription in this book that really made me very interested in actually reading it. He saw me as a strong black woman! Wow! It made me decide to at least have a look inside. Rather than reading the first page I opened the book at the index. There I saw a statement that connected immediately to my thoughts and feelings.

As I started to read this book it began to give me all the 'right' words I needed to be told at that time. It answered many of the questions I had asked God, my friends, and myself, over and over again, in my head. *"Why does this keep happening to me?" "I can't take it anymore!" "All I have ever wanted was..." "Are you stupid or what?" "What is trust and what is Truth."* As the answers came, I began to gain a new understanding of myself and life. I finally realized that all along, *I* had allowed all these things to happen and it was *I* who had wasted all the time up to the point where *I* let it all happen again, which left me crying and getting stressed out. I realized, when I read the book that nothing could happen unless I put myself in a position to make it happen. I realized if I do not like something, I should simply not be around it or I should act on it, so that it cannot make me feel bad. There it was! Something so simple!

Who was really to blame for the sadness, pain and torture I was experiencing? The same experience which I had been in hundreds of times already. To tell the truth, I was scared of change, and so I stuck to what I knew, because that way I felt safer.

I discovered that if you stay with someone because of material things, and made up excuses and reasons for it, things will keep going wrong just because of things, excuses and reasons. The kids, the car, the home, or the money will never help you during your times of strife. However, it's not only women that get into this cycle. Most men look for women elsewhere, despite the fact that they have a decent woman at home, because they don't really want to be with her either. They too have one hundred excuses that they tell their friends, family, and their other women, as to why they still stay around. Some of these might be:

'It's because she's my children's mother. It's for my kids'. 'She is reliable.' Or because you are the 'mother' he always wanted. We should not, however forget the fact that the car is now practically his and a third of your wages are spent on him!

My children's father called this book my 'bible'. He seemed to get very anxious when he saw me reading it. In both a physical and a subconscious way he could see that it was causing changes in me, and how I thought, and therefore, my actions towards him. This book was teaching me to stop looking outwards at others and to look inwards to myself. It was giving me a sharp wake up call.

I now no longer cared about not wanting to be a single mother or about preserving the family unit. I no longer cared about being alone. All I cared about was me! Me! Me! I had had enough.

Three months later I left him for good. He tried to hang around me for a while, but my mind was set, and there was no going back.

Do not for one minute get it wrong and think that it was so easy. There is nothing worse than really hating the relationship that you are in and wanting to leave, but knowing that your heart is always going to give you that *warm sensation* every time you see that person. I could not escape the fact that he also resembled the late Tupac Shakur, and that formed much of the attraction. However, I realized that the same feeling of warmth towards him would only last for two days and I would want him gone again. I prayed to God to take away the feelings I had for him and to keep me strong.

I had to write myself notes and stick them all around the house, reminding myself of all the horrid things he had done to me. 'He spat on you Maurisha!' 'He steals your money Maurisha! I had constant conversations with myself regarding my own importance and the love for myself over my love or lust for him.

I constantly went over self-trained procedures for not opening the door to him and I erased his number from my phones, making it as difficult as possible for me to call him. I also gave up the role of the dutiful *'baby mother'* and stopped attending family functions and get togethers; although my children still had contact with their grandmother and extended family, and on occasions when asked I was happy to send them.

However, despite the families pervious get rid or put up and shut up advice, the decision I had made to finally fix my problem myself caused a stir. I was called a bitch for not letting him see the kids, a bitch for not attending special family occasions and last but not least a mad bitch because I stuck up for what I believed, and one by one we began to fall out. All because of 'my MOUTH' or so they say.

It was hard looking after three children on my own, without being angry that he did not give a penny or a damn, now that there was no house, no car and no other benefits for him to gain. But I learned that it was okay to be angry. I had to learn not to give him or them my anger, so that he could use it to tempt me back into the circle of bitterness. I learned to deal with my problems and feelings myself, by recognizing that he could not **do** anything, apart from cause more issues for me.

Great! I had done what I wanted to do; I had conquered a change in my life. It felt good; in fact it felt great, but only for a few months. One day I was faced with another challenge: that of being alone. I had no **male** companion; every girl's greatest fear. I spent many nights crying and many days walking around in my own world, feeling hurt and bitter. I decided to stay strong and fight, referring over and over again to Iyanla's book. It told me to cry if I wanted to, that it was ok!

I had always had an interest in martial arts and decided to take up Shaolin *Kung Fu.* I spent four hours every Sunday learning form and techniques, kicking, punching and breathing skills. I noticed that I felt fresh and rearing to go every Monday morning. Life was not that bad at all! All that I had feared about being separated was actually not really that awful, in fact, it was the best I had felt in years. What I did not realize at the time, and have since discovered, is that my interest in Kung Fu at the time was more than a coincidence. Martial arts have hidden truths behind them. These truths concern our true capabilities and power over our own minds. What I was actually doing during Kung Fu was releasing my stressful, negative energies: *anger and hate,* with every kick and punch, and, in turn, cleansing my thoughts with breathing and stretching exercises. Through practice and determination I was able to do things I had no idea I was able to do.

During the rest of the time I kept occupied as much as I could, bringing my three children along with me everywhere I went. I spent a lot of time visiting friends. Some days I would return home and other days I would stay over, depending on how I felt at the time. I did not have to rush home to attend to a hopeless relationship that was freedom!

Luckily, or should I say coincidently, my younger sister was with her first, teenage boyfriend and regularly volunteered to baby-sit for me as long as her boyfriend could come along. So I had the opportunity to extend my socializing to raving, as well as visiting my friend's houses.

Great! I had achieved an important mental change. Next to be dealt with were my emotions. At first, I despised any man that came next to me. I believed that all men were dogs and vowed never to go there again. Besides, I could not see any 'good man' wanting me with my, *'one bag ah pickney'*.

At first, my line would always be, *'I have got three kids...'* but, to my surprise, this did not seem to bother them. One man once said to me, *'We are all big people now, who does not have kids?'* I realized, again, that there was nothing to be scared of after all. However, I remained sure that I did not want to enter into another relationship, with a man, for a long while and placed an imaginary cage around my heart to protect me from love and the issues that seem to come with it.

I began to socialize more and more. I found myself smiling, feeling good about life, laughing out loud - until my belly hurt me – again, actually feeling good about me. I found myself releasing the anger and bitterness and balancing it with happy, affirmative and positive feelings.
I no longer felt hatred towards my children's father and just accepted my past with him as part of an experience I did not

want to enter again. I felt that I now knew how to deal with such issues.

One morning I woke up, got out of my bed and stretched, like I did every day. However, this stretch felt different. I went to the mirror and stared at myself for a long time. I actually said, out loud to myself, 'HELLO!' I was actually happy to see myself! I then realized, in a way that I had not before, that it was really all over. I had done it! All the babble about inner-standing yourself, knowing your self, loving yourself, over-standing yourself and so on, that had been preached to me by many different types of people, over and over again, I now understood and *I had done it*!

Not only did I find the power to leave a bad relationship but I had also found myself and the power in me. What I did not realize at the time was that I had achieved this a long time ago, but had not known it then. Where I was now was just the beginning. I moved forward in a new light, I had found myself *or so I thought!*

5 It was all meant to be

I got myself a job in my children's school at lunchtime and took a short child minding training course. Upon completion of the course, I set up business as a registered childminder. I was strong, and had confidence, and it radiated throughout my life. I promised myself, should I ever decide to be in a relationship, that my partner would have come to me because he truly wanted to, not be there out of any form of *convenience*. He would treat me just as I deserve, he would be romantic, fun, and sociable. I did not just say this to myself casually; I fixed this within my mind and had faith, with all my heart, that I would accept this and nothing less.

In May 2003, I met a man who is now my ex-partner and guess what? He was just that man!

We had been associates for a number of years then we became closer friends, in regular contact, for approximately two years before we became intimate. We would regularly see each other at local food shops, night clubs and more generally in the locality. We would call each other and moan about our domestic issues, new men in my life, his baby mother and our respective kids, as friends do. I was not completely unaware though, that, given the fact that he was a man, I needed to be fully conscious of what his underlying wants might be. He brought these up one or two times in funny, cocky gestures but he showed me respect at all times.

Some time into our relationship he broke up with his partner, and he looked to me for friendly advice. As friends we began to see each other more frequently, as some men always seem to need a woman to call on, so they can ask 'one hundred questions' a day. It doesn't matter either whether that woman is their girl, friend, sister or mother; they just seem to have this need. One day he came to my house to pick me up to go for a drive, when I got into his car he had the radio on a station that, at that time, was playing lover's rock. The instant I heard him sing along to the music, I saw him in a different light.

I have always loved music, especially *old school lover's rock*, *revival, rare groove* and *culture*. They remind me of the 'good old days'. I had made it my duty to get all the *old school* songs onto CD and play them every Sunday, whilst boiling my peas, just like my mum had done. On that occasion in the car, I turned to him and said that I did not know that *breddas* like you listened to this kind of music. He simply looked at me straight in the eye, smiled, and replied, *'I'm not like any bredda!'*

We talked for hours about life. I saw a different him. In fact, I was impressed, more impressed than I had been with his fancy car, flash clothes and money. I wanted to see more, more of this different him.

I invited him around to mine one Friday evening for a drink, we listened to music and talked all night and to my delight, for every selection of music I played from 70's reggae, 80's pop, 90's *slow jams* and up-to-date *culture*, he sang along to them all. From this day onwards we were inseparable.

When we first got together it was heaven. The energy was high, infectious and visible to anyone who came around us.

He was sexy, loving, kind, fun, generous, spontaneous, sociable, and a family man. He would take me away for romantic weekends and spoil me rotten. He would clean the house, cook dinner and relax my hair. He had three of his own children and was a wonderful father to them and brilliant with my kids. I truly felt that I had it all. Most of all he was a leader, someone who took charge of himself and did not *leech*, or depend on, other people to do things for him. If there was something he could not mange himself, he would pay someone else to do it for him.

Within three months we were living together. We went everywhere and did everything together. We shared what we always thought about but had never got around to sharing before. We inspired each other and those around us. My friends and family were so happy that I had found someone to treat me the way I deserved to be treated.

He did, and was, everything that I could have ever wanted and most importantly what I asked for although it took me three years into the relationship to realize this. Spiritually, I knew it all along, but my ego could not handle it. I got what I wanted but I forgot to say what I did not want. You see, he came disguised as the most cocky, confident, charming, fun, charismatic, loving, demanding, self centred, arrogant, angry, beautiful chocolate-coloured Black man!

Within the first few years we discovered that, we had so much in common it seemed unreal. We decided to get engaged. Things were good, so good, it became 'too good to be true', that we both started to wait for bad things to happen, and guess what? They did. We began to argue over every little thing. At first it was over male friends calling my phone, then his baby mother, my baby father, his kids, my kids, cooking the dinner, his friends, my friends and so on and so on, interminably.

Through each argument I reflected back to my 'strong black woman' spirit. It demanded that I do nothing other than what I wanted to do and if he did not like it, then, well he should leave. I refused to get caught up in the cycle again. Each time I came to the conclusion that thinking and caring about me, above all, was the right thing to do and I refused to take on board his issues or feelings. However, whenever I weighed up our relationship, the pros always appeared to outweigh the cons. He would leave and we would get back together, he would leave again and we would get back together again.

By this time I had two part time jobs, one working in a nursery, which my mother owns, and the other working for social services. I was also enrolled on two college courses: one in British Sign Language and the other in Management in Childcare. I still had to run the house as well as maintain and provide for my three children. His constant need for conflict, attention and resolution became too much for me. I wanted to do what I wanted to do, when I wanted to do it and I did not want to have to answer to, or do, anything that others wanted me to do.

I became convinced that we were not meant to be. Only this time I was not scared to leave. Or so I thought. Yet again, the pros seemed to outweigh the cons. However, this time it led me to question my own self and whether my strong black woman thing was actually right, either for me, or in reality. Could it possibly be right to leave someone who does everything one loves and only a few things that one hates? It did not make sense, so I decided to stay until I was absolutely sure. We would regularly argue, however the 'love' seemed to get stronger and stronger.

6 She who feels knows

One day, my ex came across some black history information on the net, which made him curious about life. He would often try to show me but I was always busy doing college work, cleaning or shouting at the kids. Until one day I was deeply betrayed by a long standing friend whom I had known for 13 years. I was very hurt by what she had both done and said. I swore to God that I was going to find out why life was like this. I was sick of arguments, pain, hurt, spite and hatred. I wanted to know why people do the things they do.

I picked up the Bible and started reading Genesis. The first place it speaks of is the Garden of Eden and its rivers, followed by the name of its dwelling place and to my surprise, it is ETHIOPIA also known as Cush. Well I never... Africa! Wow! I read on. As I did so, it all sounded lovely, but made no actual sense to me and it certainly did not answer my questions.

However, since the Bible itself spoke of Africa, I decided to take interest in the information that my partner had been trying to show me all along.

I spent the next four years, day in, day out researching. Each area of study led to the other, revealing the answers to each and every question I had about life. I looked into history, language and literacy, sciences, including astrology and medicine, geography, politics, yoga, holistic health and healing. I also looked into palmistry, star sign astrology, numerology and other strange phenomena such as physic ability and clairvoyance. I studied various cultures and religions including Christianity, Islam, Judaism, Buddhism, Hinduism, and Rastafari. This finally lead to ancient Egypt and present day African culture, along with the so called *Occult Books* (I prefer to call them **o**ther peoples' **cult**ure).

There was finally a meaning to life for me. There was finally a reason; a simple reason for every little thing. At first, I wanted to write straight away. In fact, I had written right up until *this paragraph*. Then, I got stuck. I knew just what to say but I did not know how to say it. I wrote fifty pages of straight hard facts, but somehow feeling that it was not quite right. The people I wanted to tell have a strong tendency to *not* want to read. They appear to not like to learn and certainly don't like to listen to anything other than music!

I gave up and a few months passed by, but I had the intention of completing it one day. I continued life in my new-found, positive light. I undertook a course in crystal mediation and herbal medicine and began to offer my services to those around me, sharing my wisdom and guidance in any way possible. I successfully completed my child management and sign language courses and gained new employment working as an 'appropriate adult', assisting youths and those with mental vulnerabilities in police custody. Months later I enrolled onto a combined Honours Degree in Criminology and Psychology at university. I continued to study and learn so that I could still continue to gain and grow.

However, the more my ex and I began to grow, individually, the more we began to grow apart. As I geared my life towards the embrace of my people, he focused on his wants and needs in the relationship, but for his self. As I would sit chatting all day long, inviting people around for knowledge and meditation sessions in between my job, the house work and the children, my relationship began to crumble. No matter how hard he tried to show me, I felt that what I had to do was more important than his selfish need for me to fulfil his 'fairy tale' relationship. This was one in which the woman sits at home, all day, living every breath for her man.

One major ammunition factor was of course MAN. Despite the fact that I accepted all of his female friends and even let the mother of his eldest child sleep at my home with her children, he could not come to terms with men calling my phone, coming to my house, or even me talking about them, for any reason. I put it down to insecurity. What I could not, at the time, see, is that he too had feelings; he too had an opinion, wants and wishes, just like me. So my reply would always be what he used to call 'rude', and not what a man should be hearing from a wifey. He would always say it was not what I was saying; it was how I was saying it. This was something I have often been quick to tell people but could not see in myself.

Eventually, we decided to take a different approach to the relationship, so he moved out. At first the space was great. It also meant the fact that as a man, now in his own flat, that he would get to finally see what it takes to run a home: cook his own diner, wash his own clothes, change his own bedspread, pay all the bills and do all the shopping (not just hand over the money). He would learn what it is to sit in the housing office for hours and get messed around by the gas board. Then, perhaps, he would see how much I did do for him.

On one hand it was a good move for me. On the other hand, as the sound of wedding bells became a distant noise, I began to realize that I had something I had asked for, something I had wanted and could not even see. As I received love I wanted to be alone again. I had received love but never loved love. How selfish! Despite his bully boy, inpatient, arrogant self, along with the skeletons in his closet which I think he needed to address, I had someone who would have done anything for me. I needed to take a harder look into myself. But after taking three years to realize this, it was way, way too late. As my granny would say, "it (had) dun spoil".

Despite my efforts, the privilege of our own space, and the fact we had learned so much about the balance of life's ups and downs, the arguments became more and more frequent.

Until, one day we I had an argument, one which changed my life. This argument was unlike any other, this was the end... the end of us. I could just feel it. As he walked out of the door, for the final time, I knew better than to sit at home stewing on the argument, causing more negativity within myself. So I decided to write my feelings down.

I remembered my friend, Nicola, telling me that she wrote her feelings down in the form of poetry, so I thought I would give it a try. Three months, and a lot of writing later, there it was! My book! Through coincidence after coincidence, I finally found a way of saying what I wanted to say and had been trying to find a way to say all along.

It was not only the end, it was also the beginning. Maybe it just had to go this way. But yet again I was faced with breaking free from my 4 year relationship and the bonds of love. We carried on seeing each other for eight months or so until, eventually, our relationship was over. He would always say that my mouth was a major contribution to both the negative and positive aspects of our relationship. Sometimes, I agree with him. Or at least I agree that I could have handled situations differently. But hey, it takes TWO to tango.

I do admit however, that I walked into the relationship thinking that I knew it all. Not knowing that I never really knew who I was, I never really knew where I was going and I never really knew what love was. I learnt that whatever we choose for positive reasons will always come accompanied with things which we perceive in a negative light. The choice is not about right and wrong, the choice is about whether you can view things from a balanced perception or not. Whether you think you are just you, or whether you understand that you are interconnected to the universe. I never knew that the thoughts I manifested in my mind could determine my whole life. I never knew that whatever I imagined I shall receive. But most of all I never knew that I create my own destiny with the choices I make, to the extent that I do now. This time it was not learning about how to control relationships and my feelings. This time it was about how to control my whole life.

I leant that I am not just me. I a combination of my genes, my ancestors and their experiences, my life *and* my experiences, and a little of each and everyone I have encountered along my path.

I am My Mum, her confidence, strength, ambition, pride and constant love towards her child... *"I am now that Mother".*

My Step Dad, his cooking, his strength, his compassion for others... *"I am now of that essence".*

My Grandmother, HER MOUTH, her struggle, her love, her existence...*"I am now that woman".*

Sonia, her MOUTH, her knowledge of self, her truth... *"I am now that woman".*

My mum and her friends getting dressed to go raving... *"I am now one of those women".*

The child pretending to smoke... *"I was that child and am that smoker now".*

The one who so badly wanted to drive... *"I was that woman and I am that driver now".*

My aunty Sandra, for the way she cooked, plaited hair and looked after me ... *"I am now that Aunty!"*

The women who wanted to find strength to leave a bad situation... *"I am one of those women!"*

That woman who thinks she is nice, *"I am that woman".*

My sistrens, their struggle and their pain. *"I am one of those women".* African queen! *"I am that woman!"*

One thing's for sure is that throughout the duration of my life my mouth has always been a focal point. I noticed that my words really get to people, whether it was by being frank some call it 'rude', standing up for myself, encouraging people, being empathic or giving advice. Eventually, my path lead me unto the understanding of the power of words, knowledge and understanding.

PART 2

If only they could see!

"Life is simply about choices
Listening to the positive or negative voice.
Open your eyes and you will see
Everything is just how its suppose to be"

1 Reality – If you can't hear you will feel

I thought I knew it all,
Then I found out, I knew nothing at all!
Now that I know where I am from
Through new found vision and intellect and wisdom,
I have a new, Divine way
To say what I have to say.

Knowledge of Africa is where I learned about life
Revealing all the questions I had about my strife.
The philosophy I hold is not only about colour
But about pride in where we come from;
Knowledge of our Divine nature, and of who we really are.

I have chosen to use a form of communication
To reach out to those struggling in the 'black nation',
Those who don't like to learn, read or listen,
And therefore always learn through harder lesson.
We are all here to learn at the end of the day,
But we don't always have to learn the hard way.
This is knowledge I now live to share,
For without my race of people,
Neither I nor you could ever be here.

My brother and my sister
It's not just the youth in this generation
Who learn from their own false interpretation,
Adults who grow the children are responsible for them.
By sitting around cussing, fighting, pointing the finger
And waiting for people to do or give
We become the destruction of the lives
That our children seek to live.

In reality, through ignorance we are the only ones
Who will suffer, if we don't stop.
Spreading negative vibrations out to each other.
I am part of you and you are part of me,
We're a universal family,
But, until the day we all open our eyes
And rise together in unity
We will never, ever be more than this:
'The poor, black, ghetto community'.

2 **Reality** – Who is to blame?

Life is not just down to an individual
Choices are also influenced by you and me.
If only you could see, what I see
The REAL....Reality!

Brap! Brap!
The sound of the big man's gat! Why?
Because, big man had to defend his big chat.
So, he pulled out his big ting,
And shot a man, the guy's mother and her sistren.

But, it's not his fault, I don't blame him.
You see, he was never taught about the system
Of life, truth and the REAL reality,
He has no overstanding of his black man mentality
In comparison to generations of black men
Throughout history;
Malcom X, Martin Luther King Jr, Marcus Garvey,
The consciousness of men such as Tupac, Muhammad Ali
Sizzla and Bob Marley,

He can't see the light, much less the vision
And that the All is affected by his decisions.
He can't see that it's 'One small step for man
But a giant leap for mankind',
He can't see that he's playing into the hands of the
Inventors of jealousy, hate, anger and bad mind.

You see,
He has no real overstanding of his self
So how can he understand what he causes to someone else?

He's not in touch with his spirituality,
He lives a physical life, Delusional, blindly.
Trainers, clothes, weed and a flashy car -
If only he could see the bigger picture -
If only he could see his inner power,
Know his roots and be in tune with nature.

He would be that strong, proud, Black man
Trust me, If only he could just see Reality.
So, 'he who is without sin, cast the first stone.'
I think it's a sin we forgot our REAL home,
Ourselves, our people, the sun, the sea and soil,
Mother Africa our gold, gas and oil.

While he's killing his brother
We're sitting here leaving our people to suffer.
Making no efforts for our land, our riches, ourselves,
Always pointing the finger at someone else.

My people!
Until African people find their own mind
There will always be more Black men of his kind

3 **Responsibility** – Parenting

So called dad
One thing I never had,
Still, I never turned out too bad,
Because I had a step-dad you see
Another man, who was prepared to take care of me,
Because my biological father was far too busy.

Busy making more and more children,
And developing his skills for manipulating women.
He lived with not a few,
If I work it out,
Counting all my brothers and sisters, without a doubt.
There are now roughly around 22.
Twenty-two brothers and sisters!
More than I have toes and fingers!

My Dad says...
"Your mum and me didn't get along,
- And he is always singing the same old song -
"I've been there for all my children, from start to end,"
Or so he goes on telling his friends.
However, I somehow have a different story
Of this so called father and his
Sperm Donation Glory!

Through his own illusions,
He comes to his own conclusion.
'Tell me Dad...
To not know who I am,
Was that also part of your plan?'
"Maurisha, you have always been well"

Not that he *actually* did anything to support that,
He could just *tell*

"Dad I'm not a child anymore..."

"Yes dad, I'm well
And that was down to my mum,
And all she has done.
That can't wash on me now, dad
Because I am now one - A mum!
With my own children.
Now I'm older, now I can see,
That there was no excuse for no time for me.

You were not there to see me in hat and coat,
Waiting for you at the window, wanting to cry
Every time it was not you,
When that car drove by.
You were not there for my school journeys
To get me first in line for the coach, nice and early
You never took me, or picked me up, from school
You never bought my uniform, or
The countless pairs of shoes I went through.
None of them were bought by you.

You never bought one winter coat,
Always crying you were broke.
You never nursed me when I was sick
You were far too busy with your ****!"

Your list of excuses goes on and on
And for these same reasons, dad,
My *baby father* is now gone.
I'd rather struggle on my own,
Than have him call me on the phone
Always wanting, asking, something,
But never regarding how his children are doing.

To be a man he does not have a clue
You know what Dad?
When I see him...
I see a subliminal reflection of you!

The dad I never had,
The answers I tried to find,
You see, I never realised
I... magically, magnetically attracted it
With my mind.
So...God gave unto me
My baby father you see.
So I could discover for myself the reasons
Why you were never there for me.

"The sins of the father..."

Excuse after excuse about argument
When the truth is: you made yourself the target.
You just could not be bothered
To take care of your responsibilities;
Because all along you knew my mum, or step dad,
Would do everything for me.
Now that I'm older, it all makes logical sense
Why would you spend a pound,
When you didn't have to spend a pence!

Through him I see
You got yourself caught up in that 'can't see' game,
Always thinking everything is ok
Believing that everyone else will see it the same.

It's now become a fashion to be that distant father
Reeling out a thousand excuses about your
'Baby mother!'
Leaving their sons nobody,
Destined to become their father's carbon copies;
Sleeping around *breeding* lots of women,
Believing it's okay to not mind their children.

But Dad! I am not sad,
For my brothers and sisters I'm truly glad.
Their mum's kept us together from the very start
And trust me dad until the end,
We will never part.
We all share the same perception and story
Of your sperm donation glory!

Maybe all that you have done
Is part of a higher plan,
In giving divine existence to every, single one.
For this dad, we are extremely thankful to you, for sure
In fact, it's one of the reasons
Why we don't have to worry anymore.

Through each other we remain strong,
Not having to worry about why we didn't have a dad -
And what we did wrong.
Now, not one of us have time for you.
Imagine, we've all got better things to do!

But, Dad!
If I had just one wish
It would be for you to wake up and see
That along the paths of your lessons you have been selfish
Your lack of Self meditation
Is affecting a whole, new generation
And if you looked into yourself
You would see that your doings
Do affect someone else.
Just a little of your precious time,
That would have been just fine.

As you were the one chosen by the most high to be my Dad,
I'll tell you why you *oughta*!
While you live your life, I can testify,
The sins of the father
Are also passed on through another man
Unto your daughter!

4 Responsibility – The truth behind motherhood

Mum! Mum! Come! Come!
Tell Jayden, he won't give me one!"
"Why can't you two just share?"
"Muummm! Now he's pulling my hair!"

"Come on, now we're late for school!
Skye! Take off that jumper, it's not uniform!
Jayden, they're not for school, take them off your feet,
And don't forget to brush your teeth!"

"Coats on and let's go,
How time flies by, I just don't know!
Sit back and put your seat belts on."
'Muumm!' "Yes? Now, what's wrong?

Shut up! Sit down! Stop arguing! Stop hitting!"
'Muuumm!' "Yes Rio?
What do you mean; your book bag's missing?"

Walk the kids to the gate
Now, get to work, I'm really late
Oh my god, I hate this job!
J.O.B: Just over Broke, this life is a sick, sick joke.
This is not what I want to be,
This can't be my destiny,
Or am I being dramatic?
Oh gosh, look time to leave, I must beat that traffic!

Time to get the kids from school,
"Mind my car! You silly fool!"
Great, I'm here on time,

"Hi Naomi! Oh, I'm just fine!"
"Hi Skye! How was your day?"
"Tarah's not my friend, but I don't care anyway"
"What about you Jayden, how was yours?"
"Fine... but I did get sent to the office
For kicking the ball at the doors."
"Rio, my baby, did you have fun?"
"Muuumm! My friend had some sweets,
And did not give me even one!"

"Hush... come now, let's go home"
Ring! Ring!
"Who's that now, on my phone?"

"If only someone would have told me..."

"Muuumm, I want to be a singer!"
"That's nice darling, now mummy has to start the dinner."
"Muumm, Rio spilled his cup!"
"Ok, now you two stop talking and eat your dinner up."

Now, is this how I left my kitchen?
Why is it that my kids never listen?
"Yeah, Skye, You say you don't mean it,
Yet you never manage to clean it!"

"Listen, the thing you broke cost money!
The way you lot behave is not even funny.
Come on now, leave it, it's time for bed!"
These kids are driving me mad,
Sometimes I just wish that I was dead.

Now I've got a headache and need a pill
But not before I sort out that gas bill...

"Muuuuummm...!"

Finally, I can get some time to myself.
Time without having to do for everyone else!
Ring... ring... ring...ring!
Just as I thought I got some peace!
I find out that after many years of trying my friend
Just found out that she may never be able to conceive
And through the same illness, her mum is now deceased.

In one way it was very sad,
But strangely, in another, I was really glad.
It opened my eyes and helped me to appreciate
All the things I thought that I had come to hate

Muummm! Muummm! Muummm!
I thank God for every single one!
And even though I may sometimes feel as though
I'm experiencing strife
Really, it's just part and parcel of the gift of Life!

Contribution by Skye

5 **Responsibility** – The choices of fatherhood

You say you're a good dad,
And expect everyone to be glad
That you take care of your responsibilities
And deal with your 'yout dem' equally.
But, my brother, do you
Have to *constantly* put that child before you?
Constantly have to do things
You don't, at that time, want to do?

Dealing with siblings, fussing, fighting, and arguments
Along with those, 'just won't listen,' childish temperaments.
Sorting out who said what, punched, kicked, or hit,
Even when you're in the bath or on the toilet!
Being woken up every morning out of your bed,
With constant nagging, and bothering in your head.

My brother do you have to work around school times and
holidays,
Not forgetting parents evening and assemblies,
Pantomimes and sports days?
Having to leave work because
Your child's ill, or had a fall,
Or perhaps an appointment
At the dentist, doctor or hospital.
Constantly giving your boss excuses,
Hoping, and praying to God, he'll save your job
And you won't lose it.

Constantly feeling fed up
And still having to wash, cook, and clean up.
Without a doubt,

Stuck in the same place, day in and day out.

Anywhere you want to go
And anything you want to do
You can't, unless
You can find someone else to stand in for you.

"Child maintenance..."

You say you're broke
But, to a baby mother, that's a joke.
When a baby mother's broke, it's not even funny
There's no gas, electric, shopping or dinner money.
No money for football, dancing or treats,
No biscuits, crisps, magazines or sweets;
No money for books, games and toys,
Shoes, coats, or hair cuts for the boys.

Need to get away?
Yeah, right!
There's no chance of finding spare money
For a holiday.
Can't even buy a new pair of shoes or trainers,
Have to pay the nursery fees
And childminder retainers.

Have to replace everything the children break,
Not forgetting repainting
Every pen mark on the wall they make.
Broken videos and scratched CDs and DVDs.
Every torn book and tape borrowed from the library,

Have to provide a home for a family.
Including cooker, fridge, beds,
Wardrobes, dressing table and a settee.
Television, computer, and stereo;
Every pot, pan, knife, and fork,
And every blind for every window.

"Being a parent..."

It's not just stress, and issues financially
It's also about our children's destiny.
A woman can do all she can,
But, she cannot teach a boy how to be a man.

When you grew up, my brother, who did you look up to?
And was there anything you saw 'everyone' doing
That you did not want to do too?
You hid it from your mum, so she did not have a clue,
What was she to do?

My brother, like your mother,
Your child's mother is busy,
Making life comfortable for everybody,
While you sit down, and hope for the best,
Believing your child won't follow the rest.

Your child's mother needs a bigger house,
But has to stay in a council flat.
Three kids in one room
And don't forget the cockroaches and the mouse.

Your child has to play outside,
So from the ghetto life they cannot hide.
Bound to the council estate,
By the future possibilities his or her parents helped to create.

"Fatherhood...."

You see,
There are a few brothers in the community
Who look after their children financially.
Yet they still know nothing about love, respect,
Honour, trust, pride or family,
Brotherhood, and unity,
And this our children can clearly see.
So they look up to gangs, and thugs

Who stick together, and even die for each other
Side by side,
No matter what, when, who or wherever

Even though we adults believe it would put a stop to our
Culture's commiseration.
If the youths of these days showed a little more
Respect, and consideration,
I say, perhaps we should all
Learn a few lessons from them,
Maybe it would help to solve all our problems?

6 **Responsibility** – Children of this generation

Kids of this generation
Are lost, through our lack of self meditation.
What else is it we give them to see,
Apart from struggling, hatred and poverty?
Killing – ourselves - to make money
Then, we wonder why they
Watch the luxury hype on TV.

On a financial wealth graph of statistics
Our culture's mark is pathetically unrealistic.
We have no self confidence to reach for the very top
We're satisfied with any old job.
Believing life's harder, because we are black,
When that's not actually a matter of fact.
We have no factories, shares, empires,
Franchises or private estates,
Because we are a reflection of that which we create.

It's easier to blame others and everything else
Than it is to be true, and to look to yourself.
We are all to blame and responsible
For all of our culture's strife and troubles.
And unless we show our children great stature
They will continue
To want to become gangster rappers
Unless we show them peace, love and unity
They will continue to want to ruin our communities
Through what they see as the 'right' way to be.
Believing too
That others are in control of their destiny,
And the only way out is the one that's 'easy'!

"Watching our culture slowly die..."

It is through that same African strength, pride and will
That we are able to rob, steal and kill.
Just like those who do anything to make financial wealth
Despite the fact that it's detrimental
To our survival and health.
There are those who manufacture
Pharmaceutical drugs and chemicals
Instead of using nature's
Natural herbs, spices and minerals
There are those who make weapons of mass destruction
And a variety of everyday guns,
Instead of creating devices
That will unite us all as one.

Funny, those who mean us no good
Never sit down, and wonder, if they ever
Could, should, or would?
They gather other minds alike
And strategically plan how to implement their fight.
Whilst the so called righteous sit down everyday
Waiting for the hero or saviour to pave the way,
Continually telling ourselves ignorant lies
Watching our culture slowly die.

7 **Being Black** – The ghetto

Everyone wants to point the finger
Then run away from the ghetto
Not acknowledging that it's us that made it so.
Blind to the fact that
You can 'make it' all you like
But, you'll never fit in and you will never be white.
You will always be associated with one of your kind,
Not because of the colour of your skin,
But because of your state of mind.

While other cultures stick together
No matter what, when or however.
Black people make money
And spend it all on clothes, flash cars and jewellery.
Those that get one, good job
Lose their heads and take it way over the top,
Looking down on the brothers and sisters,
Acting like their shit don't stink,
And they don't get corns or blisters.

My Black Brother, my Black Sister
Black is not me, you or them but who **we** are.
Even though you have your own identity,
I reflect you and you reflect me,
As long as being black is part of our destiny.

Life's about pride, confidence, and personal power
Which also includes your divine origin **and** skin colour.
In order for us to fit in, along with everyone else
We too must first learn to love ourselves.

8 Being black – To know where you're going you need to know where you're coming from

You see,
Through knowledge of our Black history
You too would be proud of how black used to be.
You'd be proud of our forefather's generations,
Rulers, and creators of great inventions:

Such as:
Garret Morgan, 1923
And the invention of the traffic light.
Dr Patricia E. Bath, 1949
Who invented the first laser eye surgery
Which has given the blind sight.

Dr Daniel Hale Williams, 1891
Who performed the first successful heart surgery.
W. H. Richardson, 1899
Who invented the baby buggy.

Robert F. Flemming, 1886
And his invention of the Guitar.
L. A. Burr, 1889
And the invention of the lawn mower.

J. L. Love, 1897
Who invented the pencil sharpener.
Granville T. Woods, 1884
And his invention of the phone transmitter.

Alexander Miles, 1867
Who invented the elevator.

Fredrick M. Jones, 1939
Who designed the motor.
T. Marshal, 1872
Who invented the fire extinguisher.
J. W. Winters, 1878
And his fire escape ladder.

George Washington Carver, 1896
And his peanut butter.
J. W. Smith, 1987
And the lawn sprinkler.
Burridge and Marshan, 1885
And the typewriter.

J. Standard, 1891 and the refrigerator
Along with the inventors of
The toilet, the stethoscope, the gas burner,
The stove, the curtain rod and the mobile cellular.

"Black history..."

So close to slavery
Yet our forefathers still managed to achieve!
Despite the fact that education
Was not widely available for black people,
Until the nineteen sixties.

Even though they're gone,
The lists go on and on.
Great African kings and queens
That ruled over hundreds of provinces and countries.
Great warriors such as Shaka Zulu,
Yet many black people don't even have a clue
Of what our ancestors and forefathers lives mean
In relation to everyday life and ethnic minority individuals
Such as me and you.

The bible says the son of God, Jesus
Has hair like lamb's wool and brown feet burnt like brass.

But what we don't learn in bible class
Is that Malcolm X, Martin Luther King Jr
And Marcus Garvey.
Also sacrificed their lives, for you and me.
They too were
Strong in faith and true knowledge
Which they were taught by our ancestors to believe.

You create your own destiny
You can be anything you want to be.
Others, including our own, may believe
We don't do right, fit in or belong,
But it's our duty to prove, not only them
But also ourselves, wrong.

9 Being Black – Gangster

You're not a gangster,
You're just an ignorant fool.
Ignoring your inner strengths and power
Relying on only that of your steel tool.
Big, yeah, in the ghetto,
But to the rest of the world
You're not known.

"Don't hate the player, hate the game"
You say, yet you can't go anywhere
And use your real name.
Constantly in and out of the police cell
Hoping and praying, this time, you'll get bail.

Top shotter, Topa, Topa, tell me,
Why do you bother?
Why would you rather rob or shoot your Brother?
Why not be a proper, pharmaceutical drug doctor?

Tell me, what is the reason for your existence?
Besides death, money and prison visits.
Surely there is more to life
Then all that bullshit and all that strife.

"Just think..."

Gangster, deep in your heart
You have dreams and aspirations.
Yet, not knowingly, you choose to live
By others people's perceptions.

Perceptions of the one
Who said you're a boffin or a fool.
If you did all you could to do your best at school.
The one who lured you into the area mob,
The one who said you're a fool, if you got a job.
The one who never told you
That your Casanova reputation
Would have you, once a month,
In the disease clinic reception.
Now my brother where is he,
Living in jail? Mad? Dead?
Or at church giving his testimony?

Now... your way out you try to find
But, nothing else will come to mind.
For 'hard' you do not know
Because 'easy' is where you always go.

It's easy taking someone else's things away
Than, "fucking working hard all day."
Easier doing hard time, eating porridge,
Much easier than going to college.
Easy to sell drugs, and to be quick on your feet,
Than to strive to become that barrister
Solicitor, or banker, on Wall Street.

"The reality is..."

Here is something you don't know
Because they never told you about how it really goes.
Now, let me be realistic
Gangster, you're just another statistic!
Just another on the graph,
Just another brother who has lost his path.
The only way you see great stature
Is to become a famous, gangster rapper.

Your lack of education
Is part of a history of oppression, and manipulation.
And you don't want to be that African man
Who is wrapped up in the opponents' game plan.

Wouldn't you want to make real money?
That your great, great grandchildren's
Children could get to see?
Can't you see, Gangster,
You're not really being all you can be?
If you really knew yourself,
You would know that your Mother Africa
Is the source of the whole world's wealth.
For, where your ancestors were once sold
Is filled with natural
Oil... Gas... Diamonds, and Gold.

There is where the money is, you see,
Where you're originally from!
But the last place **you** would want to be;
For if you knew your history,
You would mess up the opponent's game plan
By fulfilling your real destiny.
But you continue to live in the world of delusions,
And your gangster 'thing' is just an illusion.

Knowledge *is* power;
And trust me it pays, by the hour.
They say...
"Anything you don't want a black person to know
Just put it in a book."
Because they know, Gangster
You ain't got time to look.

Gangster, to win someone
Your intellectual level must be greater
Or at least the same!
And, my brother
You are the **joker** in *this* game!

You need to realise that
You're affecting more than just 'someone else'.
You are all our kids can see
Growing up, and now, wanting to be
Acting like they're really bad;
Collecting stars and stripes for making money of no worth.
Going to jail, killing, and making people's families sad.

If only you could see past your flashy car,
And strive to be who you *really* are.
No matter what you've heard
Illusions are not the same as the real world.
You see hard work as LONG
But my brother, you are truly wrong.

Pretend you do not have to worry
About impressing all who you can see.
What would you really do, gangster?
And who would you really be?
But, most of all, would you have the guts to be different
And the balls to dare
To take that long haul up those steep, hard stairs?

10 Being Black – Ugly

Not only do our men compare
Women by the clothes that we wear
Size of our bums and complexions of our skins
You also call me Dark skin, Black bitch, or Black ting
And I call you Red skin bitch, Coolie or Browning;
And, don't forget those who are bitches
Just because they're fat or because they're thin.
She is making comments about what people wear,
They're judging who's better
By the length or texture of their hair.

Can't you see what has happened to us?
At one time
Neither of us black bitches was allowed
To sit on a bus.
Back then, when black people were strong,
Holding hands, singing unity songs:
Holding their heads up high,
And shouting out really loud
The last thing in **our** minds:
"I'm Black and I'm proud!"

"Proud to be black?..."

In this generation every girl wants to be
Everything but themselves
And just like the girls they see on MTV.
Burning their scalp to make their hair straight
To ensure they keep their fashion up to date
Weave, wig cap or glue on,

Anything to look less black and more European.
Everything their eyes can see,
They forget themselves, and now want to be.
Some are so wrapped up in what they are seeing,
They no longer care about their children's well-being.
All of their clothes are designer wear,
Yet, in regards to their child's education
They really don't care.
Some sisters even use bleach,
Desperately searching for 'inner peace'.

Tough on the outside but inside so insecure
Don't know who they are,
What they're doing,
Or where they're going, anymore.
Believing if only someone would love them,
It would solve all of their problems
Ignorant to the fact that
Beauty is in the eye of the beholder,
And self confidence is what they need
To make them feel stronger
You can still be natural and look like a 'hot gal,'
And unless *you* are proud of **who** you are,
No one else will see past your so called Ugly colour!

"Ugly...!"

My sisters, if you knew your history
You would see how it used to be.
Our ancestors were queen-like and kingly
And proud that their hair was naturally kinky.
They did not need hair or nail extensions
Beauty shone out of their inner aspirations.

Women can waste money
On cosmetic or plastic surgery
Only to see
They'll have a fake body, a debt,
No man and *still* feel ugly.

Perhaps they will be approached by fine men
Each and every day,
But only one or two of them are ever worth it
And none of them will ever stay.
For ugly is way down deep inside,
It's something you can never hide,
No matter how much you pretend
That ugly feeling will show in the end.

It's not a man they need to find
It's the state of their incurable
Confused, unhappy mind.
You see, God made the outside's duty
To reflect that of the inner beauty.
So, if you see ugly when you see your real self
No matter what you do so will everyone else.

11 Woman 2 Woman – Women like you

My sister
I'm speaking from experience when I say
Women like you
Just don't have a clue
What you cause for women like the new me,
And why black relationships are not the way
They're supposed to be.

All of your insecurities
Make it difficult for women like me,
Because you allow men to treat you any old way,
Despite all the lies and excuses
You'll do anything to make him stay.
Constantly taking him back
Allowing him to change the truth from your mind,
Even when you know that it's 100% matter of fact.

A home, food, money, car, sex, child after child...
Desperately anything you will give;
Hoping and praying that one day
It will be you he really settles down with.
It's ok with you if he doesn't mind his child,
Yet, white women like that
You will rarely ever find!
You can't be bothered to run him down,
You would rather sit and suffer,
Believing all you are is a *'baby mother'*.

So our men think we're all alike
And want to give women like me
All that bullshit and strife.

So, when women like me have something to say,
We're seen as mad,
Because women like you don't carry on that way.
They call us 'argumentative bitch'
Because we demand respect, voice our opinions,
And won't tolerate punch and kicks.

You see,
While you do anything just to have a man
You're forgetting to respect and love yourself,
As much as you can.
Forgetting your womanly strength, pride and dignity
That God buried inside of every woman:
Women like you and women like me.

For without a mother, grandmother,
Sister, cousin or aunty,
Along with the likes of women like you,
And, women like me
Think, where would our men really be?

"If every woman had a voice..."

My sister,
If every single one of us women had a voice
Our men would no longer have a choice.
But to return to the way it used to be
In our motherland country:
Our men carried themselves as kings,
And treated us as African queens.
They respected that a king has to come from a woman
To enter into this world.
To them we were more precious than diamonds,
Emeralds, rubies or pearls.

They could clearly see how God intended it to be
The womb of man... **wombman,**
The Queen!

Right now,
The strongest currency carries the queen's head
And queen size is the largest size bed
But, besides things such as beds and money
Without the queen bee there would be no honey.
Without the Black widow spider there would be no silk,
Without the cow, there would be no milk.
The queen is the highest piece on the chess game,
But our brothers are not
Intelligent enough to see it the same.

So my sister while you ignore yourself
And let it continue,
Generations and generations
Of lost brothers will do the same too!

12 Woman 2 Woman – Wifey

Quick, sharp, and stand to attention
The expectation of
An answer or response to every question.
Who's that on your phone?
What time are you coming home?
What have you cooked for me?
Honey, can I have a cup of tea?
Babes, can you set my bath?
Or perhaps fulfil some other, so-called 'wifey' task?

No more gatherings
With your friends and relatives,
Because it's now a place, where **he** lives.
He likes peace and quiet contained in his space
And doesn't want your people dem in his face.

No matter what time he is asleep,
Everyone in the house is expected
To silently whisper and creep.
You are expected to come off the phone
Anytime your man comes home.
You are expected to wash, cook, and clean for him,
Without constantly calling him,
With your insecurities about where he has been.
You are expected to not moan about his mates,
And how many times a week he comes home late.
You are expected to smile when he comes home,
Even though he did not answer his phone.
You are expected to sit up all night with worry
While he strolls in the next afternoon,
Without so much as a "sorry."

When he's done nothing all day
But watch football
You are expected to do it all, and say nothing, at all.
You are expected to single handedly
Make a simple disagreement
Never turn into a five day argument.
You are expected to always hold your mouth
And without doubt, always back down
And never scream or shout.
You are expected to know he needs his space
Not by actual words, but just by the look on his face.

You are expected to respect him as the head of the family,
Yet you still have to work and worry about money.
You are expected
To forgive his mistakes, and stick with him,
No matter how long, or what it takes.
Never mentioning them, ever again
No matter what, where, or when.

You are expected
To be considerate of his life's direction
And not demand all of his time and attention.
To take responsibility for your part in his destiny,
In assisting and inspiring him to be all that he can be.

"Wombmen..."

Basically, your feminine, womanly,
UNCONDITIONAL and LOVING perceptions
Hold the key to the destiny of life's direction.
A woman should always act like a woman
And not like a man,
Because a man is not designed
To do the things that we can.
We have been made and blessed with the title 'wife'
The divine reflection of a male egotistic life,

They say out of Adams side came eve, his help,

Meaning he could not possible do it himself.
Eve did not come from the foot of man,
But, his side, to help him, live, learn and understand.
They say Eve was the first one to be tricked by evil
Yet it is men who choose to rule the world
And rob, steal, and kill.
They're the ones who are best friends with the devil!
Living day to day selfishly and egotistically
And out of tune with their feelings, intuition
Spiritual love, and femininity.

"Woman deh ya more dan man"
Some say its all part of the higher plan,
Beside every good man is a good woman!

The power of a woman men truly do agree
Which is why they call their precious
Ships, cars and guns **She!**
To bring forth life she was the chosen one.
To embrace the struggles of our people
Then it was Rosa Parks Now it's mothers and guns.
Because *he knew* without her UNCONDITIONAL LOVE
The power of Most High can never be done.

13 Woman 2 Woman – Respecting him, is loving you

What is it my brother,
What do you want from me?
What is it?
Please tell, I just can't see.
Why do you keep on calling me?

I like you and you like me,
Is this all our relationship is ever going to be?
Brov, I don't want a wedding ring,
But I do deserve something more, than just a casual fling

I'm sorry, but I can't continue in this way,
Causing my wants, and my needs, to pay.
I don't mean at all to be selfish or a bitch,
But I also have a life to live.
You see, how you worry about your wealth
Is how I treasure, love, honour and respect myself.

In order to respected your wishes
I need to ask you questions about where this is going to go,
But the truth is my brother I don't think you even know!

I think you're stuck in an illusion
The place of no true conclusion,
Can't find no way out, can't make any sense,
Let alone start find a solution.
And whilst you're acting all the time
Like the big, tough guy
You're ignoring all the come backs
Of your inner-reflected lies.

"Baby mama drama...?"

Answer this question...
Am I just another girl, on your players list?
Tell the truth to yourself,
Think now... Can you really be honest?
Where did you sleep yesterday?
At your Baby mother's house?
Had no choice. Scared she'll take your child away?

If that's the case, it seems simple to me,
Why don't you go and make a go at that happy, loving family?
Or has all your inner confusion removed your courage to try,
And behind them big, brown, beautiful eyes
You hide behind exclusive excuses and make do lies.

Never looking to yourself,
Always blaming something or someone else.
'Because she, if she or...
'I don't know what happened,
The relationship is just not the same.'
Wake up pimp daddy!
Headache comes with the game.

If, like you say,
It has become too much for you to bear
Then, her feelings and chance of happiness
With someone else,
Surely you would truly spare?
And, if where she is, like you say,
Is not really your home
Why are you there when you're not here,
Because you're scared of being alone?

My brother, being alone is not such a bad thing,
You don't have to commit or answer to anything.
You won't have to live your life a lie
You'll never make another innocent girl cry.

"Is it me or her...?"

Ask yourself; find the answers to this question,
Are you scared to make that final decision?
Not for me or for her, but for you,
And your heart's intention.
And will your own vision, along with your own needs,
And your own wants,
Be the reflection of that decision?

You see, my brother,
Why I have to bother?
The truth is not just technically for me,
But for all-round relief and respect for everybody.

14 Relationships – We need to talk

Hello?
Yeah?
Hello... are you there?
Go on...

I need to talk to you,
I don't know what to do.
It's not like before,
And I just can't take **this** anymore.

What do you mean you can't take it no more?
Listen babes, I don't know what to say,
I said I'm sorry...why all this ... today?
Did you not get the message I left on the phone?
It's straight to the point, no fuss, no joke
And I said it without having to moan.

Why when we argue do you walk out the door,
Why is it you just can't stay, and talk some more?
I need a resolution, or some sort of conclusion
Unlike you, this means more to me
Than friends, or raving or money.

What do you mean, the problem is me?
I can't stay; I can't talk, for me it's much easier to walk.
Talking to you is not easy
It's like you're talking straight through me,
It seems like you're talking to you.
When it's like that, I can't take it
And that's the door I choose to go through.
Babes...I'm not being rude,

I'm not that kinda dude
But honestly Maurisha, can't you see it my way too?
Walking through the door won't solve a thing
It won't help us stop arguing about every little thing!
In fact it solves nothing.
Communication is the key to a relationship,
So you better start talking, if you want us to make it.
Rude, my dear, is not your middle, but your first name!
And one reason why our relationship's is just not the same.

"You never listen...?"

How can you say that with all your back chat?
You're a this, you're a that and all that crap!
That's why I do what I do
It's why I don't rush to talk to you!

So you stay at your mums' for three days
And think when you come back everything will be ok?
I must sit here alone
While you jam with your friends and don't answer your phone?

The very next day, I asked you to say
Exactly what's bothering you.
You didn't wanna talk, you preferred me to walk,
And that's the kinda thing you like to do!

"That's your perception..."

That's your interpretation,
Made from your perceptions.
Darling, don't forget the day before
When, yet again, you walked through your famous door!
Should you have stayed that time and listened?
You would have understood what I really meant,
And we would not be here at this moment.
Anyway, this is long,

Everything I do is always wrong.

You will never admit
That you are also part of it!
I don't care anyway,
Don't wanna talk anymore;
I got better things to do with my day.

You phoned up my phone
To do what – moan?
This is what I have to go through,
Say what you've got to say but, at the end of the day,
I'm someone and my opinion counts too.
What is it you want? What can I do?
Maybe it's me, but you're just not getting through
I said sorry, I meant it
But you're just being pedantic
I'm starting to think it's long, too...
Are you trying to draw card? Make it deliberately hard?
Or is this what all women do?
Don't wanna talk no more
Yeah, I said it before
Now, speak to me and not you

"What do you take me for...?"

Whatever, my brother,
I'm not your baby mother!
I don't know who you think you're talking to!
You men, just ain't got a fucking clue!
Funny, you would listen to me
If I was skinning out my p****!
Furthermore come off my phone,
And furthermore, this is no longer your home!
I just can't be what you want me to be,
I will never see what you want me to see

Baby mother, p****,
Leave my home, and you men just don't have a clue,
Listen to what's coming out of your mouth,
Is that what's important to you?
If you take away all the frills
You'd know what I want from you.
Your interpretation, perceptions, and all your past
transgressions
Have an influencing factor too.
Babe, if you'll listen one more time,
With the exception of taking me into consideration,
All I want is you to be you!

"Maybe I was wrong..."

It's not that I don't love you,
But what else should we do,
I just don't have a clue.
I'm sorry, I do admit
I did play a big part in the argument.
Just promise this is the last time,
And everything will be fine.
Now, seen, as it's so,
All this is long, dinners ready,
What time are you coming home?

(Contribution by Seth)

15 Relationships – You complete me

You were that flashy guy,
The one who catches everyone's eye.
Short in stature, tall in confidence and pride
With a somewhat surprising, charismatic charm
No girl will ever easily find.
But still I could not see, never had a clue,
That all along
I was destined to be with you.

We bumped into each other at nearby locations,
And phoned each other for friendly advice sessions.
As a friend, you were always there,
But of the real, true you, I was not aware.

Finally, came that day
I began to see you in another way.
Just that simple day we spent together,
Even though I saw you many times before
On that day it was made clear to see
You were all I asked the Divine for, and much, much more.

Afterwards, I changed my perception,
I hoped and prayed that our relationship
Would change its course of direction.
After the first time we made love,
My God!
It was then that I knew
That you were definitely sent from above!

I often lay awake at night, staring at you,
Wondering if it was really true.

This was a different kind of love,
One I never knew:
The love that I had experienced before
Was an illusion,
Now you walked through my door.

You have done more for me
Than anyone ever has done:
Holidays, gifts, jewels and support
The list could go on and on.
That family man with my kids;
You do more for them, than their dad ever did.
You are there for me in every way,
Know how I really feel, no matter what I say.

"Years later..."

Imagine, many years on,
Our relationship is still going strong.
Side by side, like Bonnie and Clyde.
We made it past the good times, bad times,
And all those who bad-mind us,
All because our relationship is built on
Loyalty, love, respect and trust.
It was no coincidence.
From that very first moment
You came into my destiny's path
To be my spiritual, soul mate,
And my physical other half.

God knows I'm not easy,
Still, you go out of your way to please me.
Baby, you are my rock
And, loving you, I'm never ever gonna stop.
I thank the divine for the day he opened my eyes,
And made it clear for me to see
Baby, you complete me.

16 Relationships – Lost without you

I understand it was me who kicked you out,
When you wanted to talk... I wanted to shout!
They say if you love someone you set them free
So, if it's real love, you'll come back to me.

Now I can't sleep worrying what it will be,
Whether you feel the way I do, or, now that you're free
You're living your life without me, *and* you're happy.

I'm scared to death to even tell you,
I'm scared it's not what you want to do,
I'm scared that me and you are really through.

But in order to make things clear
I'm gonna have to face my biggest fears.
I'm gonna have to fight my EGO.
I'm gonna have to let my heart flow.

Babes... I really love you,
Are me and you really through?
Should I sit here waiting for you?
Babes, after all we've been through,
Please just tell me what I should do.

No pressure, I just wanna know,
Do you still love me?
Are you still mine, or should I let it go?
Whatever the answer, then, let it be so.

If the answer is yes,
I swear, babes, I'll try my best.

I'll consider your feelings.
Your perceptions, your actions. and your reasons.
I'll take control over what I say.
I'll consider saying what I want to say, in another way.
I'll consider things you want me to do
In order for this relationship to make it through.

17 Relationships – I'm through

If you don't take time to communicate with me
Calmly, patiently and willingly;
This is how it is always going to be.
You never seem to want to reach an understanding,
Rather, just realise the negative emotions you're feeling.

Each and every little thing
Recalls things from the past
That are supposed to be forgotten.
So we can't get to deal with our future
Because our past is still a problem.

So, this time, no matter what you do or say,
This time, keep it that way.
Walk out of my life and stay away.
No more need to consider me,
Be sad; **feel** angry, abused or unhappy,
No more going through
All the things you say I do to you.

I'm sick of fighting a losing battle
The fussing, the arguments, and the struggle.
Constantly trying to prove,
And finding more and more parts of myself
Which you wish I'd remove.

To maintain a relationship with you
I just don't have a clue.
It's seems as though
Nothing is good enough;
No matter how hard, or what I try to do,

So I give up, I'm through!
"I wish…"

I wish I could change,
I wish I could be what you want me to be.
I wish I could see what you want me to see,
But, I acknowledge, I wouldn't be me.

I wish you could do
All the things I want you to;
But, I acknowledge, you wouldn't be you.

I wish you could see all that I see,
But, I acknowledge, you wouldn't be you,
You would be me!

I wish I could always say
The right thing at the right time;
But, I acknowledge, that would be according to
Your thoughts, feelings and experiences
And, not mine.

I acknowledge that when I did those things to you
I did not have a clue.
Things I go through to learn my own way
Will affect you - the way that they do.
I do not do them intentionally,
Spitefully, selfishly or bad mindedly;
I do them because I am me
Learning and growing in my own way,
Little by little each and every day.

I can't change what happens, or how I feel,
But I can change what I do about it and what I make real.
The only thing I can do now is make a brand new start
Because, I acknowledge,
I can only change my future, I can't change my past.

18 **Relationships** – Love

Everything is new at the start
As you are accepted for who you are,
Before the relationship gets to the emotional part.
Everything is wonderfully great,
Everything is cause to appreciate.
You're constantly glad,
As opposed to being constantly sad.
Constantly smiling at the phone
As opposed to sitting home, upset, alone.

From the moment you fall in love with a woman - or a man -
Things suddenly change in line with the expectations,
And the masculine and feminine game plan.
You can no longer be yourself
Because now you **belong** to someone else

You are expected to accept all of your partners
Issues with you:
About every little thing that you do.
Whatever the problem
You are expected to always change to suit them,
And no matter what you do or say
It's not seen as real love,
If it doesn't go the other person's way.

"Misconception..."

The thing we call expectation
Is a big ego misconception,
Causing a great deal of confusion

Between unconditional love
And insecure emotional illusions.
The relationship will never be what you want it to be
As long as you believe
If you really love someone
You have to do everything to make them happy.

You are not expected to do any, and everything
Even things you don't want to do,
In order for a relationship to make it through.
Other than be patient, loving, understanding and kind,
Taking into consideration
The perceptions of your partners mind.
And as long as you ignore this 'divine' rule
Relationships will always seem cruel.
It is the insecurities and expectations of her or him,
That requires the need to know
Everywhere your partners going,
And everywhere they've been.
Convinced your partner
No longer has a need for platonic friends,
Because of the expectation that
They'll sleep with them in the end.
Through faults you find within yourself
You expect, it's only a matter of time before
Your partner runs off with someone else.

"Conditional love..."

If you can't learn to respect and appreciate
The person you're with, for who they are,
Whether you're a man or a woman,
Your relationships will never get very far.
Self insecurities will prevail
And one by one
Your relationships will desperately fail.

If you believe you can **change** someone else
You will find you're only hurting yourself.

Because true love has no set conditions,
As men and women are divine reflections.
If you want someone to stay
The last thing you do is to push them away.
By wanting them to be everything you want them to be,
Insisting they agree with all you can see.
People don't like being treated this way
And tend to no longer want to stay.
Feeling unappreciated,
Gives them a reason to want to stray
And the perfect excuse to
Not turn that new girl or guy away.

19 **Just being me** – I ain't easy

For some reason my Brothers just can't seem to handle me.
They say me I'm trouble you see...Me? I ain't easy.
But Who am I?
A strong, black woman, travelling through my destiny,
But on the other hand, sit back and I'll tell you what
spiritually.

My brother, I'll tell you why you can't chat to me,
But please excuse me, you may think being I'm being rude,
cheeky or feisty,
But just ask around and chat to other people and they'll let
you know,
Why my mouth is "ever ready and good to go".

Spiritually, you see
I view myself as a queen, empress, a goddess
And I'm always trying to strive to achieve my best,
I'm always trying to find ways of taking care of my people,
By spreading peace, love and unity, not wickedness and evil.

Physically,
I got three children, I raise on my own.
So, my brother I really ain't got time for you taking up my
phone.
I also have a job and go I to university
So, I don't need your sweet talking, or your money.

You see my brother it takes a lot to please me
Because I love me and I'm not the average black gal with man
insecurities

And I'll tell you what my brother no matter what you think
you're on....
I know that what I'm on....you just ain't ready, and soon
you'll be gone

You see you ain't ready for the power of my mind relayed
through my tongue.
Because the only power you possess is in your pants, or, in
your gun.
But you see, what I got between my legs
My brother, let me tell you ain't for little ignorant, foolish
tegeregs!

Bwoy, you're the one who better can cook! You know
Do you think it's really all about your name brands,
And your pretty looks?
Your 'big gun' and 'making man shook.'
Who's got the best left or right hook
Every gal yuh si hafi tek ah juk...PLEASE!

I believe women should be treated as equal,
Which means, anything a man can do...'she can also do too'!
Anything you say my brother, I'm gonna say something back.
Now, tell me do you see that as 'back chat'?
And when I'm expressing my feelings on the phone
Would you hang up, and sort it out when you get home?
Or would you listen carefully, willingly
Loyally, intensively and lovingly?

Tell me my brother, would you have insecurities about me
talking to men,
Despite the fact that you have platonic girlfriends?
Would you be cool with my 'fam', and my socializing?
Or tell me would you be male, egotistically dominating?

Would you understand that I'm learning in my way,
Growing little, by little, each and every day?
So it's guaranteed there will be times I may not do or say
What you want me too, my brother or in your way.
Then Would you think it's ok to hit or hate me,

Just because you're insecure and not balanced emotionally?
And can't you see you're simply feeling hurt and angry
because your love my brother is based conditionally?

Do you think it's okay to blame everyone else,
And never look for blame within yourself?
You ain't ready for me, trust me,
Cause me, I ain't easy.
My brother, if you don't know who you really are
My brother if you don't acknowledge your divine nature,
The Earth, the sun, the moon and the stars,
My brother, don't even bother.

However If you can see what I see - reality -
And you're not bound by the spell of leviathan and sleeping
beauty,
You'll too see the **African queen** in me,
And you'll know just why. I ain't easy.

20 Just being me – Sorry

How can I be sorry when I did no wrong?
Before I say sorry, I'd rather be singing sad songs.
Sorry is for the weak and not the strong,
For I am right and you are wrong.

But, I wonder, should I wake up one day
And see it from your eyes, in your own unique way,
Would I then have something different to say?

With no knowledge of my mind and for my reasons,
If I put myself into your position, in response to my actions
I too would have taken offence,
And developed similar feelings.

I now see that,
Wrong can be right, and right can be wrong,
And for this simple reason, you could be gone.
This makes no sense to me -
I'm sure on this - you too would agree.

Wrong and right can be seen in two directions
Somewhat like a mirror reflection.
So If I say sorry, I'm not admitting wrong,
Just sorry about the fact that we're not getting along.
Sorry that my point of view
Seems somewhat different to me,
Than it does to you.

"I'm sorry..."

I do admit, sometimes, through the mist and pain,
That there are hidden parts we do not wish to unveil.

I understand now, should I have said these things to you,
It would have perhaps given you more
Overstanding of me, and, the things that I do.

It's not that I don't love you, or mean you harm,
It's just that...
When people don't understand me,
My mind just can't seem to remain calm.
The confusion and illusions
Draw me to all sorts of conclusions.
Then, disguise themselves as hurt, and pain,
Not realising that right there and then
I had everything to lose and nothing to gain.

I'm sure you have experienced this feeling I'm explaining,
That emotion that takes over your whole being,
That was not there in the **beginning**.
'It was not supposed to go this way,'
And, 'that's not what I had meant to say.'

Although, through it all
I learnt a wonderful lesson.
And one thing we do have in common
Is that, no-one remains the *same* person.

'I'm sorry' does not mean we may not disagree
On another occasion.
However, I promise to always remember
The key to misconceptions and communication.
And should it be at the point I can no longer stay,
I still want to say it anyway...
I'm sorry.

21 Without you – Just what I need

Weed, weed, weed,
You're all I need.
Without you to make me happy
I don't know where I would be.
No one else can do what you do for me!
You're the only thing that would make me
Spend my last money.

You're so beautiful and kind
The way you inspire my mind.
The way you make me feel so relaxed
I no longer go to work or pay tax!
I'd rather be with you, buzzing and laughing,
Sitting around all day doing nothing.

I need you so bad;
Without you, I'm sure I'll go mad
When you're not around
I can't keep a smile, and feel really down.
You are the answer to my every question,
You assist me with my aggression
You keep me company when I feel lonely,
I don't need a man, you are my honey.
You will never sleep with my friends:
You will be with me there until the end.
You will never shout, or argue, with me
As long as I keep getting high and spending money.

When your love wears off and I no longer feel strong,
I can dip right into the bag and build another one.
You'll always help me get by

As long as I keep spending my money, and keep getting high

"The question is...?"

The question is,
Weed, am I your one and only?
Weed, am I worth your last money?
Weed, do you love me as I love you?
Am I that special?
Is your love for me illegal too?

When you're with me, can you think straight?
Do you constantly put things off
Until another date?
Do you forget the simple things?
Do you no longer feel inspired to do anything?

If the answer is no,
I'm sorry, I'm gonna have to tell you to go -
I know you will always be there.
Baby, you know this relationship does seem a little unfair!
You see,
Weed, I would die for you, can't you see?
The thing is, this,
would you die for me?

22 **Without you** – Friend

I'm on Self Destruction Street,
Can't see a clear road ahead,
But I can see my feet.
Where I'm going I just don't have a clue
Just passed Self Pity Lane,
Now I'm taking a left on Breakdown Avenue

Of course that's not the way I'm trying to go,
But, without your direction, I just don't know.
I'm walking down Try Your Best Close
But direction is the thing I forget the most.

I just want you to text me the address again
To Don't You Even Dare Lane!
I know you got your load,
But, I'm just getting to
Get up and Wash Your Skin Road.
And without the rest of the directions
I just don't know what to do.
Please, when you get a minute,
Just text me the details,
Even if I have to go through
Cuss Me Off Avenue.

(Contribution by Nicola planter)

23 Without you – Beloved

Whenever I'm down, whenever I frown,
You're always there
With your angelic, tender love and care.
You listen to my babble,
And guide me through mistakes
No matter what it is, or how long it takes.

You know the difference between
My ego and my real self,
And you always know how to help me break down
That negative, mental health.

Always got time for my story
Through man worry,
Kids, bad times, and all the glory.
Somehow you always seem to know
The things I hide inside.
And don't feel no way to make me aware
Of too much pride,

You got my back when 'I don't have a pence.'
You always find a way to make me see sense.
Beloved, if only you knew
How much you mean to me!
Without you, I do not know where I would be.
That day you were given life,
Was to help me balance out my strife.
All along it was meant to be
You and me, throughout history.

Should we share the same Mum or same Dad?

For the day that they made love, I'd be extremely glad.
And should it be that we're not even related,
I'm extremely glad, anyway, for the day you were created.

Sometimes I'm so wrapped up in me
And the straight road you help make clear, for me to see.
I forget to say
Thank you, for what you've done for me. Yet again! Today!

Don't forget, you too
Can let me know
If there is anything I can ever do for you!
My sister, my brother, my friend,
I'm there for you too, right 'til the end.
It's a blessing knowing you, beloved,
And just remember God made me too
To keep your back covered.

24 **Without you** – Rest In Peace

Tossing and turning with pain inside
The day I heard the words that you had *died*.
Sweet memories of you,
Oh God, if only you knew!
Should I have known
That you would not be here today,
I would never have said the things that I **did** say.
I took it for granted that people will never pass away,
And there's no coming back, no matter how hard you pray.

Your kiss and your touch,
How I miss them, so much.
Your face, your smell and the texture of your hair,
I miss your cussing, the fights
And your 'don't ramp with me' glare.
Christmas times, and special occasions,
Your rice and peas and your roast potatoes!
Oh, my God, your apple crumble!
Why couldn't I just have been more humble?

If only you were here to see
The woman you grew, and made, of me.
And the man you made of my brother,
Mum, to us, there will never be another.
You have three grandchildren now, a boy, and two girls,
Only wish they too could have had you in their world.

Knowledge and words of wisdom, now I see,
All of which you were trying to teach to me.
I'm sorry, my mum, my friend, my other half,
Last time we were together

I was lost, and, still finding my path.

I added to your stress and worry
And for that mum, I am truly sorry!
Although I cannot kiss you,
Until the day that I die, I will always miss you.
And although your face I can't physically see,
You'll always live, inside of me.

(For Tomika)

25 Happy – Wanty wanty cyan getty getty and getty getty nuh wanty

Whenever you make a decision
It is always wise to use wisdom and intuition.
Don't be deluded by your eyes,
Because the grass is not always greener
On the other side.
It all depends what time of the day you're looking
And the position in degrees the sun is in,
Because everything you get or do in life
Always comes with something.

Yes, it's nice achieving things in life,
But not for one minute will it end your strife!
Egotistic material things please you physically,
But they will never help you emotionally or spiritually.
Beware of which state of consciousness you choose,
Whenever you're judging yourself against others,
Or making a decision of what's right for you.

Once you actually get that man
You'll soon want him out of your destiny plan!
Once you get that pretty girl
She'll be sure to destroy your heart,
And wreck your world.
Once you have a baby
You will see how hard responsibility can really be.

Once you get that big job and more money
The more bills and debts you'll accumulate,
It's not even funny.
Once you get that car

Without petrol, tax, insurance,
MOT and breakdown cover,
You won't get very far!
Then, they'll produce a new model,
Next summer.

Once you get that new DVD, stereo or big screen TV
You'll need insurance, in case it breaks down technically
Then, they'll bring out a newer version,
In the sales in January.
Once you get expensive jewels and diamond rings
Ignorant people want to rob, and steal your things.

Once you get that house
You'll have **the** neighbour from hell,
And perhaps some garden slugs or a mouse.
Once you reduce or increase your size to fat, or thin,
You'll find you need a new wardrobe
Of clothes to fit in.
Once you go to the hairdressers
To make your hair shiny and straight,
You'll find you're already thinking about
The money for your next appointment date.

Once you have 'whole heap' of friends
At least one of them will chat you,
Or stab you in the back, in the end.
Once you become a famous celebrity
You're the perfect victim for the paparazzi.

It's not just about what you got or get
It's about what you're gonna have to do.
So next time you choose
DON'T act like you don't have a clue.

26 Happy – I ain't got time

I ain't got time to watch you,
Because I got better things to do!
I can't fulfil my destiny
If I'm always watching you,
And never watching me.

I got no time to live in your past,
Wasting time to my future's path.
I ain't got time to watch
What people do with their privacy,
It's not feeding my children or paying my bills for me.
I'm so happy with my life,
I ain't got time to give anyone all that strife!

You see,
I only wish you were as happy as I am,
So that you can use your precious time
To achieve the best that you can.
You too would have a car
If you could see past me that far.
You too would have that man
If you were not wasting time,
Involving me in all your jealous plans
People would respect, and love you too,
If only you would be yourself,
And stop watching all that
I do, or don't do!

"You've got better things to do too…"

You see,
If it makes you happy watching,
Or putting down someone else,
You're clearly not happy within yourself.
You don't have peace of mind
And happiness you find hard to find.
The truth is:
If you were really happy
You would have no time
To watch or chat anybody.

So, I say a prayer for you,
And ask the Divine
To guide you in everything you do,
So that you can use your time wisely
And be just like me.
I ain't got no time to want to
Follow the hype on TV!
I am over-content with being just me!

No time for hype, jealousy, hatred,
Anger, or stress,
Only time for that for which I have been blessed.

27 Happy – No!

We tend to live two lives:
One inside, and one out.
One real, and one fake, without a doubt.
Sometimes it's hard being your real self
When relating things to someone else.

Just simple things throughout the day;
Doing to please others,
Never saying what the real you *wants* to say.

Sometimes it's hard to say no,
Even though you really don't want to go.
Sorry, No! You can't use my phone!
No! Sorry, I can't take you home!
No! I don't want to take you there,
You know what... I really don't care!

Sorry, I don't want that responsibility!
No! I don't want to lend you money!
Sorry, no, I can't give you some,
Even though I have little and you have none.

You know what, I just don't want to talk.
No! I don't want to give you emotional support.
No! You can't borrow my car!
No! You can't come for dinner!
No! I don't want to sleep with you!
No! That's not what I want to do!
No! I don't want your bullshit and strife!
No! I don't want to live this kind of life!

"No!!!"

Think!
Can you,
Will you,
Could you,
Feel guilty
About what is really meant to be?
And all you're not allowing
The other person to see?

You see,
The real you knows, that 'no' as well as 'yes',
Are divine, survival lessons
Of dependence and independence.
So, by always saying yes
You're not always helping yourself,
Or others achieve their best.

NO! Is not just a word
In the dictionary,
As well as yes!
No! Was also meant to be.

28 Happy – I can't take it anymore

You say
You don't deserve to be treated this way,
Yet you choose to stay.
You say,. there's no compromise
It's always his or her way, or nothing.
No matter how much you try
He or she has always got you up for something.
You say He or she treats you like a fool,
Yet, you stay, believing one day, you'll wake up
And everything will be cool.

You say, He or she communicates
With other women or men,
So, you're convinced they'll do it again.
Maybe? Break your heart,
Just like the girl or man did to you before
Who was there one minute,
Then walked out the door.
Not realising that you were convinced
It would happen from the very start,
And not admitting that
You entered into the relationship with a bitter heart.

Through your insecurities you have no time for self
Always pointing the finger
At someone or something else,
You see,
You are not them and they are not you,
So what is in their mind,
You don't really have a clue.
How they choose to live their life

You judge from your perception, as chaos and strife.

"If only they...?"

You prefer to reiterate the past,
Instead of looking to a brand new start.
Wasting time moaning about your man or girl,
Attracting constant magnetic negativity into your world

You ignore what is clear to see,
You would rather live in self pity.
Convinced that there's no hope,
Feeling helpless and ugly
Worshipping the god of insecurities,
Believing its how your life's supposed to be.
Ignoring the divine lessons and clues
Of what not to accept and what not to do.

Should you decide to stay right where you are
You will learn that you won't get very far.
Things will never seem fair
Until you have the balls to dare,
Believe and trust in who you are,
Regardless of house, money, partner, or car.

You see,
Until the fear of who you are is gone
You'll stay in that dim circle and never move on.
With self trust, self confidence and love of self
You'll never have to feel the impact of free will and choices
Of **someone else**.
You will see that the things other people choose to do
Never have to bother you.
For you have a choice too,
To do what's best for you.

First weigh out the pros and the cons,
Then, decide whether you intend to be weak or strong.
My brother, you are a king and my sister, you are a queen,

And you divinely determine what is meant to be.

Through each hurdle and each test
In the forms of
Survival, health, career, money or relationships;
You will learn, ultimately
By any means necessary,
In order to gain anything else,
You must first learn how to love, trust
Respect, have faith and believe in yourself.

29 **Possibility** – The voice in me

Everything was fine, until the voice
Everything was once one perception,
But now, I have a choice.

That day I heard the inner things
I did not want to hear
That day it all became crystal clear.

The voice.

The same voice I heard in the background,
Time and time before;
Yet because the truth hurts...
I did not want hear it anymore.

So I searched for another solution,
And got stuck in the mind of institution
      I will,   I wont,
      I do,   I don't,
      I can,   I can't.
    Its right   it's wrong
    When all along...

The truth was, and is
Far more than what's on the surface.
Far more than the mere voice,
Of simply choices.

Shusshh!...
Quiet!... Listen!
It's simply, I want! Or, I don't want!

Keep your head up,
And everything will be just fine.
You'll get through like you always have,
Time after time.

The voice of truth.

These are tests for everyone,
In their own unique, divine way,
A simple thing I forgot until, today

"Easy...!"

It was he, it was she,
Is always easier than it was... me!
Good-bye, and, go away,
Is always easier than please stay.

It's easier to pollute my head with negative excuses
And negative glory,
Than to just simply look into myself
And say sorry.

'Fuck you too!'
Is just, oh, so much easier
Than 'I love you!'

Easier to take someone back
Who means you no good,
Lying to yourself
With fake reasons why you should.

It's easy being easy,
I just sometimes forget to see,
That easy
Never
Pleases
Me.

30 Possibility – I can do it

Through all the grinning and grinding,
The 'ruff' and the 'tuff'
Escaping the army of
Should have, Could have, Would have,
Through the times of the tears, and self pity,
The countless of days with no money in the kitty,
The times I was stuck in a dark ditch,
Loneliness ! What a bitch!

I couldn't see past the pastor,
Serving the God of fear as my master.
Blaming and constantly trying to find excuses;
Someone or something to pass the buck,
Forgetting it's me and not them
That is actually stuck.
Stuck in the illusion of no-way-out
My mind was convinced, without a doubt.

With eyes closed at something so plain to see,
The only thing that was wrong was
My attitude, and me.
I forgot that I had been here before,
Until it was me - I - who had the keys to that door

Should I have not been so low,
Would I have ever reached up so high?
Would I have ever realised that
My limit was the sky?

Unlike the last time I was at rock bottom,
And couldn't see the top,

This time I will get that dream man, and dream job.
This time, I'm not gonna stop.
I will get that dream house, and dream car
Overcome any hurdles, no matter what they are!

Set myself some realistic goals and tasks,
Fix up and take off the make do with masks.
I forgot who I am, I forgot that I can;
Only this time I won't forget
'Bwoy, dem nuh si mi yet!'
As I sit back, and visualise, where I will be,
I can finally be happy with just being me

"I can..."

Now it was plain to see
That was where I was.
Many times, I had previously been
Many times I did not have.
Many days were grim, grey and really bad.
When, one day, out of the blue
I knew just what to do.

I delved into the pit of my stomach
And pulled out that part of my deepest courage,
That courage I had put away,
And totally forgot that I had saved
For such a day.

Looking back on how I had grown
From last year, September
I encouraged my self to always remember.
The pledge I had made
Since 2006, December

I can do it! Yes, I can!
I will be **all** that I am!

31 Possibility – Choices

What goes up must come down.
What goes in must come out.
Left/Right   Big/Small,
Black/White   Short/Tall,
Weak/Strong   Right or Wrong.

Two sides of the brain, left and right
But when you put them together
You see the world in a whole, new light.
It's all the same at the end of the day
If you choose to look at it in another way.
If you change your perception
You would see that everything has a reflection.
After all, where would right really be
If there were no other directions?
It's one direction with a choice of left, straight or right.
One colour with a choice of black, mixed or white.
One height: short, average or tall,
One size: big, medium or small.
One strength: weak, feeble or strong,
One decision: right, not sure or wrong.

They say, spiritually you have a choice between
God and Jesus or the Devil,
I say mentally you have a choice between
Being wise, intelligent, or a fool.
How it was meant to be
It is made clear to see.
Divine balance!, the 'Universal Rule'
Of spiritual, mental and physical

"Heaven and Hell?..."

Divinely balanced in between your left and ride side
Your heart, mind and soul you will find.
You decide whether you see the world
As cruel or kind.
Depending on your state of mind
Your thoughts create feelings, which lead onto actions.
So the world you're seeing is your divine reflection.
You'll live daily in heaven or hell,
Through God's gift of freedom, and choice of free will.

You see,
Happy, laughing and feeling glad
Feel just as good as feeling angry,
Throwing a self-pity party,
Hurting someone or feeling sad.

It's just that each has its own divine reaction:
Inner peace and love,
Or hell, fury and destruction.

Ying and Yang
One whole
Half positive and half negative
And, at your will, how you choose
Will determine how you live.
You reflect your destiny
By how you create your possibilities.
In all the things you do
And how much you acknowledge
The divine balance in you.

"The universal rule..."

Mentally visualise a possibility
"Ask the universe and you shall physically receive,"
"It will come true, as long as you believe."

There is no need to choose sad,
When you can choose
To be happy and constantly glad.
Smile, and have faith.
Don't run it down, cry or frown
With divine balance,
The less longer you will have to wait.

Just as long as you, believe in yourself.
And stop searching for answers from everyone else.
You will see the beauty
In all that was intended to be.
You will see your lessons,
And the clues to your divine mission.
There are no coincidences or mistakes
They are all parts of your destiny, your fate.

But, should you choose negative to pollute your mind,
Then negativity and destruction you will always find.

"Good and bad choices..."?

No two people can have the exactly same DNA
Therefore no two people can see things exactly the same

Whilst people waste time judging
Good or bad remains dependant
On what side you're standing
No one chooses to see it from a balanced perception
No one choose awareness of the universal interconnection.

If all that was meant to be, will be
Then it was the devil's destiny
Which all started with a tree.
The tree of knowledge of good and bad
Holding the knowledge of the paths to being happy and sad
Planted by the Most High's divine hands.
God knew someone would **be lying** to **Eve**
And gave her free will to accept the one she chose to **believe**.

How could we know good, If we do not know bad?
How could we know happiness, if we do not know sad?

In order to have a choice
There had to have already been another voice?
If the devil too had an 'obey or disobey' choice
Then clearly he is not behind the power,
Behind the 'disobey voice'?

The voice of greed, jealousy, hate, and anger,
Selfishness and laziness.
Which leads to an eternal life of sadness, illness and
unhappiness
Experiencing nothing other than grief, bills and stress
That voice which could cause you to judge,
Rob, steal, or even kill.
The voice you are able to receive through the gift of life
And the power of positive and negative, free will.

32 Life – Action, Reaction

Just as the cycle of day:
Morning, noon and then night,
No matter if you think it's alright,
"What is done in the dark will come to light."

No matter how much you try to hide your pride,
It will eat up your insides.
No matter what you try to pretend,
Whatever is wrong will slip out your mouth in the end.

People say, "What goes in will come out."
People say, "Be careful what you say with your mouth."
You must not use such words as 'can't',
Or you will never get past the start.

I say
Just as so called witches cast so called spells
Your thoughts and words can affect yourself,
And others as well.
"What you do comes back to you."
Now think,
How many things have you wanted in your mind
Which have really come true?
Including those trainers or that coat,
Despite the fact that you were broke?

All you imagined as a child
Look around now,
And see how much you can find.
The home?, The children? The car? That special man?
Not knowing that back then you were already starting

To mentally build your divine destiny plan.

"Coincidence…?"

It's no coincidence when the gas runs out,
And you get that money at the last minute,
Without a doubt.
There are no coincidences
When you think of your friend,
From the vibrations they send
And then your phone rings.

But you just answer
"Hi! I was just thinking of you!"
Not really having a clue
of who you really are
And of your divine, inner power…

Don't you wonder why you have déjà vus
And why it is that
Your grandma's dreams always come true.
Why answers for years you try hard to find
Just one day pop into your mind.

33 Life – Fear

The truth hurts, or so they say
But through a fearless perception
You can see it another way.
No matter what you do or say
The truth will get its way.

Smiling in the light, on the outside,
Will never override
The truth in the dark of your insides.
Every time your insides feel scared
It won't allow your outside to explore, try, or even dare.
You will never leave that negative relationship,
Fear won't let you see past it.
You will never apply for that job,
Fear will never let you see yourself at the top.
You will keep people at a distance for protection,
Because fear won't let you see past rejection.

You will stunt your growth in wisdom,
And delay your divine mission.
You will never fulfil your destiny,
Because fear will never let what was meant to be, be

But whilst you waste time fearing
Someone or something else
Really, you're only fearing
The power, and possibilities, of yourself.

Confidence means taking risks to be
Fearful of nothing and nobody.
If you're scared you can not give your all,

Therefore you are unable to reach your full potential.
People are less likely to take you serious, or show you respect
And you become first in line for being manipulated
By those with knowledge of self, and confidence.

"Fear..."

Born into ignorance, otherwise known as
Death, or skin.
Don't know who you really are,
Or where you're really going.
But, when innocent babies learn to crawl
They have no reason to fear, or try, anything at all.
And always get back up
No matter how many times they fall.
Children are highly in tune
To their dark side, and spirituality.
They see things we cannot see
And have the ability to tune in to others'
Mental vibration frequencies.

Emotional or egotistic perceptions of life
Are not a part of children's personalities.
Therefore, they have no need to fear
Reality,
Spiritually, or physically,
Until grown adults programme them with
Fear; ghost and boogie-man stories

"Scared..."

Scared of the dark, and all that it brings,
Yet without the dark
There would never be morning.
'Let there be light,' was the first thing God said,
So prior to this God lived in perfect darkness.

God doesn't want his children to be scared,
He made the light
But the DARKNESS
Is what was originally there!

The light was made for us to see;
A learning process on earth
Through a physical perception,
And human Destiny.
The darkness will always be there;
To remind us of our spirituality.

In our mother's womb of darkness
In our purest state, before we enter the world of light.
And, nothing feels as sweet, and refreshing
As the darkness of sleep we enter every single night
Or when making love, or even praying,
And compelled to close our eyesight.

For light to shine, it must be surrounded by dark.
Which is why you'll find the truth in the hidden parts
Of your mind
And your feelings, way down deep inside
In a dark place, no one else but you can ever find.

Should you add negativity
To your great power of darkness,
You will find that you don't like it.
But, should you face your dark side,
In a positive light
Equally everything will be alright.

"Death..."

Death is reflected as ignorance, or fear.
Once you've programmed your mind against it,
The purpose of your life will never seem clear.

You see,
Death is a divine state
Of consciousness, that you create.
Once we die you don't know where you really go,
So, subconsciously you take this on board
As fear of the **unknown.**

Ignorance on the other hand
Is merely about what you ignore,
And take no time to know, or understand.
Being scared of exploring new perceptions,
Or something else,
Because it's hurts the old beliefs of self.

To come alive you must first be dead,
Just as the seed in the flower bed.
D-ealing with E-motions A-ffecting T-he H-eart
Will give you the power and push to start.
The final end,
And the beginning, of growth of something new
To make way for something else divinely in store for you.

Finally, your burdens have gone
Now those old thoughts, feelings and experiences
Are dead and buried, you have moved on.

34 Life – Awareness

Knowledge of you
Is reflected in all that you do.
And should you keep finding yourself
In the same position,
It means that you have not yet learnt your lesson.
A world of tests:
To discover the do's and don'ts
For your own happiness.

Through all that we see, hear, and have done,
We all divinely learn and grow through intellectual wisdom.
Learning the reasons why we should or should not
Do that certain thing,
By ac<u>knowledg</u>ing the reaction it will bring.

We learn general, physical <u>knowledge</u>
At nursery, primary school, secondary school
And then on to college;
To learn greater <u>knowledge</u> of us, the world
And its divided cities.
We then move on to university
We learn <u>knowledge of</u> life and emotional experience,
Through childhood, parenting,
And then becoming grandparents.

But if you can't hear you will feel,
Through ignorant of knowledge
Of what is realistic, real.

Often the things you should really know
Are in places

We can't be bothered, or are scared, to go;
Including way down, deep, inside,
Because you believe
There's no need to question your pride.

You believe you're always right
No need to face the truth, in the dark.
Rather, stay in the light.
Afraid your way of thinking might not be so,
Besides it's not the way you want it to go.
"Forgive them father for they do not know!"

"Ignorance..."

Should you open your mind
You'll be surprised at what you can find.
Knowledge of you is in everything, everywhere,
All the time.

Through everyone, and everything,
We all learn something.
Student, teacher, headmaster
Church-goer, Bishop, Vicar or Pastor
So called Witch, High Priestess or Wizard Grandmaster.
Knowledge separated in forms of clues,
For you to divinely learn all about you.

"Education..."

Knowledge is your spiritual destiny,
And coincidently, comes with high flying careers,
And financial security!
Such as doctors, stock brokers
Scientists or officials in the Government
A bunch of well-educated people
who are very intelligent.

Just think, you're dressed in a cape and hat
Like a witch or wizard,
When you finally graduate university.
With a doctorate, B.A Hons, Masters, or a degree.
A degree,
Is also used scientifically, mathematically
Also in relation to those who are able to master
The art of their spirituality.

Education holds the key to divine representations of you
In words, numbers, shapes and symbols
The stars, the sun, the moon and triangles.
1..2..3, 666, pentagons, hexagons, ovals, and circles

Knowledge of the difference between being born into sin
And divinely, biologically, being born into skin.
Knowledge of the snake,
And its 'recognition' as the symbol of evil
In relation to its being used world wide
On ambulances and by all the medical professionals.
The symbol of knowledge of our body
Known as the rod, the staff or the kundalini,
Meaning snake like or coiled, such as our reptilian brain,
Along with our intestines,
And the tiny microscopic layers of our shredding skin.

"Genius..."

There are **9** numbers between one and ten
Then they reverse back around again.
9 planets surrounding the sun,
9 months from conception to become a mum,
Cats and their **9** lives
Superstition or tales of old wives?

Each number originated from one,
multiplied, added, subtracted or division.
Such as we have done to our existence,
Cultures and religions.

2, 4, 6, 8, 10
So it shall be done in the beginning
As it will be done in the end.
1<u>2, </u>1<u>4, </u>1<u>6, </u>1<u>8, </u>2<u>0</u>
Not just mathematics, but also connected to spirituality,
So let's explore the **3rd** dimension
3, 6, 9, 12 and the divine balance lessons,

12 Tribes of Israel, **12** sons of Jacob,
12 months in a year,
12 fish and loaves,
12 disciples Jesus kept near.

$1 + 2 = $ **3.**
Jesus and the **3** in one Holy Trinity.
The Holy Koran and the **3** words: Alif Lam Mim,
The Holy Bible and the **3** wise men.
The devil and his little tricks
The mark of the beast and his **3** in one: 666.

In order to make a happy family
You need **1,** a man, **2,** a woman and...**3,** a baby.
First come **3** stages of trimester during pregnancy,
Then **3** centimetres dilated before
The woman's admitted to the ward of maternity.
3 names to the baby's identity,
3 numbers of the arrival on earth of the baby:
The year, the month, and the day.
Individual characteristics built within the child's
3 in one **D.O.B.**...and **3** in one **D.N.A.**
As the child reaches puberty
Hair begins to form in **3** parts of the body:
The head/face And armpits and places of privacy.

The Star of David,
The star of Bethlehem?
The star that guided the **3** wise men?
Your spiritual connection to the
Universal Soul: the **sol**ar system.
9 planets:

134

Even though we cannot see,
They still exist in the dark void of our galaxy.
Each one a different colour
All rotating around the big, yellow, solar star.

God's promise, shown to us in the sky,
As a colourful rainbow;
3 primary colours: red, blue and yellow.

Without colours we could not see anything or anybody.
But whether we see them, or not,
Everything has its own energy vibration frequency,
Including you and me.

Entering our body at different speeds
And reflected as all that we
HEAR, TOUCH, TASTE, SMELL and SEE;
Known to us as our 5 senses.
The **6**th "**sense**ssssss" being our intuition:
Feelings and subconscious.
So we can pick sense out of what's good
What's bad and what's nonsense.

If you believe what you're eyes see
Or that of everyone else,
You will ultimately learn to use Intuition of self.

"Wisdom..."

First...God thought; said the word
Then there was creation.
Just as our minds and words form
Our manifestations.

Man created all we see
With our imagination, awareness and strengths
Of our individual capabilities.
Along with our feelings emotionally

135

Trial and error,
And researched knowledge, scientifically,
Using only that of which God made for us naturally.

Some with a vision of love
For the ALL, and everybody.
Some with the vision of love for money.
Some with the vision of love only for those in their religion,
Race or community.
Some based on his story history
Some based on my story mystery
Egypt and its darkness
AFRICA the dark people the '3rd world' country!

Some based on technology,
The plug, 3 pins,
3 wires
Positive, earth and negativity.

Some based on the wolf, and the 3 little piggies,
Some based on the story tale of sleeping beauty.
Some based on the story of Goldie locks and the 3 bears.
But through the spell of ignorance,
The whole towns asleep and unaware!

35 Life – The universal you

Should you read the Egyptian creation story
Of Osirus and Isis
You would see they're very similar to the
Holy Bible book of Genesis.
Translated from the ancient African tribe
Of Sumerians,
Through the Babylonian, Egyptians,
Muslims, Jewish and Asians.
Then passed down to the
Greek and Hebrew.
Then translated by the western world
And then passed on to you.

They say
God decided to create the earth
Out of the blue one day.
Let there be light, then it was done:!
The universal sun!
He then sat back and relaxed at all that he created
On the 7th day
Being **Sun**day.

Just as the Holy Bible quotes
The coming of the son of man: Jesus
The **sun** resurrects every morning in the east
And dies at the west.

Amun Ra the ancient Egyptian, **sun** god
Known to the Egyptians as the true hidden one.
Muslims prayer rituals
Also revolve around the rising and fall of the **Sun.**

The Egyptian: .Amun Ra also known as Atum Re
Can be translated as sun ray,
Not forgetting <u>Amen</u> each time we pray.

Whilst we ignore others values
And argue over a simple name
Each religion's principles remain universally the same
The stars, the sun, the moon
The dark and the light
Those who do wrong
And those who do right
Kings, books and colours
Peace, war, shapes and numbers

"The Sun..."

The most breathtaking thing on this earth
You could possibly see,
Is a beautiful, hot, island or country,
And its wonderful, natural scene.
We all look forward to summer time
As the bright, morning sunshine
Has a way of making everything seem fine.
Bringing the confidence we hide throughout the year
To get married, go on holiday or face our biggest fears.

In order for all on earth to survive,
The sun
Is the main force of energy keeping us alive.
The moon is the reflection of the sun,
While the sun lights up the other side of the world
When our daytime is done;
The light and the darkness in one.

In order to breathe, we need plants and trees
But, without the sun, and rain water,
Trees could never be.
The sun heats up the ocean, the water, then evaporates

The vapours rise into the air and cools down,
Condenses and become droplets.
This then forms a fluffy, white cloud
When this gets full, it bursts
Allowing the water to soil, feeding
And cleansing the ground.

The same ground on which the animals
Graze and feed,
In order for us to have the balanced diet
We need.
Along with Sun-cooked foods
Such as herbs, ripened vegetables
And fresh fruits.

"The Light..."

The fastest energy vibration is the speed of light,
The energy from heat, depending how bright,
Also known as the colour **white.**

Red is the slowest speed of energy
Also seen in the sky, depending on the time of the day
And the setting of the Sun's degrees.

White; Angels wings, doves and halos
Red; devil, danger and lava filled volcanoes
Deep in the core of the earth,
Where you find, silver, diamonds
Rubies, pearls, gold and emeralds.

Hot **red** blood, with **red** and **white** cells,
Programmed to heal and keep your body well

To burn, fire inhales oxygen
And releases carbon dioxide,
Just as you do in your insides.
Once your heat is gone
It's time for hymn and graveside songs.

The light, otherwise known as the soul
For without it we would never be whole;
The big ball of fire of burning gas
Reflected as the candle at morning service mass.

"Twinkle in your father's eye..."

They say
Jesus was crucified for the truth and knowledge
That he spread.
I say
Now that he has gone, the resurrection of the **sun**
Is ignorantly reflected as
The son of God resurrecting from the dead.
Despite the fact that he himself said
"I'm the offspring of the bright morning star, David."
"Why are you crucifying me,
When the scrolls say, 'Ye are all gods,"
Meaning you, me and everybody.
I acknowledge that the Divine Creator
Lives within me,
And the great, spiritual powers,
And physical capabilities
That he gave unto me.
And because I say this,
You say, what I say is blasphemy?
Ye workers of no knowledge and iniquity!

Like the devil, Jesus too said;
'You too were made in God's image you see,
Ye will know yourself as a god
If only you would take fruit from the knowledge tree.'
He also said that anyone who believes in me shall do as I do
But some will not choose to use the courage and power
Because even though it's written in black and white
They still don't have a clue.

"Know thyself…"

Our ancestors taught us
That to know where you're going
You have to know where you're coming from!
Acknowledge that you too are a star the sun, the light,
God's child, a chosen one,

Hidden way down deep in your chest,
Reflected as confidence and personal power
Of the solar plexus,
There you'll find acknowledgement of who you really are;
The beauty of Divine Mother Nature
And the power given onto you by the Most High Creator.

What you know determines who you are,
And, by ignorantly,
Ignoring facts, you won't go very far.
What your mind knows
Determines how you grow.
Through the researching of knowledge and information
You too can find a self revelation.
By questioning, investigation and research
Into yourself, your world, and your universe.
By opening your mind to higher states of consciousness,
You become open to receiving knowledge
Of the life of which you have been blessed.

Just as our parents,
God knows we will learn the lessons of life
Even if we choose to live them, blindly, in strife.
He knows that
In order to see the light
You have to balance judgement on the scales….
Equally left and right.

Knowledge only of self confidence, self power,
Self capabilities and self worth
Will get you nowhere.
Too much self confidence and power

Makes you treat others in a way unfair.
Too little of something is not enough,
And too many hands in the pot spoils the broth.

He knew that
"They will turn good to bad and bad to good"
Just as we would grow from children to adults
Ignorant to wise
And learn that we should!

36 Life – Nature

You consist of:
"Involuntary actions caused by feelings"

Fire,
The candle, summer or south spiritually.
As long as you are alive.....you have hot, red blood
Running through your body.
You have a warm and loving personality,
Or, you get hot tempered, when you're angry.

You consist of:
"Emotions"
Water,
Winter or west, emotionally.
Water takes up over 70% of your body.
When you cry,
Just like the rain falls from the sky,
Water falls from your eyes.
We spend the first, nine months of our lives
In the water of our mother's womb.
There we do not use our lungs to breathe
Instead we use gills, as fish do.
In fact, the water inside a mother's womb
During pregnancy,
Is comparable to the salt water within the sea.

You consist of:
Communication
Air
Autumn or east, mentally.

Learning, willingly or ignorantly.
God blew his breath into man
And through our brain, heart, lungs, wind pipe;
And words,
We can live, learn, talk and understand.
Without the vital element of oxygen in the air,
Released from the trees.
Your brain would cease if you could not breathe.
Vibrations of energy
Work through the air to enter our body
Such as disease, hearing and visibility.

You consist of:
"A body"
Earth
Spring or north, physically.
Skin, flesh and bones.
Minerals and vitamins A, B and C,
Fruits, herbs, spices and vegetables.
Iron, copper, calcium,
Potassium, iodine, sodium.

Without the earth, we could plant no tree
And, without the carbon dioxide, man realises
A tree could not breathe.
And with no sun, or rain water
Neither tree nor man could ever be,
And you would never be able to live your dream.

You are a branch of the tree of life
And by not acknowledging nature,
Your world, and your life:
You not only cause yourself pain
Again and again.

"Nature..."

Nature has calm, loving actions
Along with those of total destruction.

144

Calm, beautiful, natural scenery
Earth quake, hurricane, hot sun, volcano,
Or desolation caused by a tsunami.

Mother Nature will be cool and kind
Anytime she can relax her mind
But any time she needs to worry
She'll be sure to cleanse the earth with storms and floods
And drench the quarries
If we continue to show no respect for our universal mother
We will be sure to feel the raft of the creator

The divine balance of nature is gone
And people walk forward blindly on
Our people are lost
And women treated unequal
And our natural traditions have been replaced
With false teachings, churches and steeples.

37 Life – Inner consciousness

Knowledge of colours, numbers and stars
Help us to understand who we really are
They help us understanding the
12 personalities we each possess,
Ruled by states of consciousness.

The number 0
An egg...round...a circle...eternal.
Darkness, Nothingness
Bringing change, transformational

The number 1
The Creator,
Oneself, the leader
Existence;
Acknowledging the soul with which you have been blessed.
All the colours of the spectrum in one.
White... peace and protection;
Divine inner peace, also known as heaven.

Pure selflessness;
The state of infinite consciousness,
Acknowledging your Divine all-powerfulness.
The crown chakra;
Your highest connection to the source.
Body function, the head, of course.
First of the divine plan
Ruled by the star sign; Aries the lamb.
Along with Scorpio, ruling the, sexual organs

Also known as Tuesday, <u>Mar</u>di, or the ruling planet Mars,
Or the consciousness of actions, courage, ego, self respect,
Self esteem and desires
Will, assertion, impatience, lust and passion
Sexuality, machismo, rage, anger and action.

The number 2
Duality.
Dependence, partnership, strength and individuality.
Violet and Dark Blue... spiritual power
And the mind's creativity.
Magnetic consciousness:
The essence of the mind and where thoughts manifest.
The plane of emotional intellect, volatility and reason,
Intuition, telepathy, ignorance, and wisdom.
Mentally weak or strong
At acknowledging the divine balance of right and wrong.
How you see the world, cruel or kind.
The plane of the universal, state of mind.

Universal spiritual love or, deluded with your eyes,
'Living' an ignorant 'death' or, truly alive.
The chakra known as the third eye
Ruled by the star sign Gemini
Two sides of the brain, left and right
The power of choice other than with the eye sight
The body part: the nervous system
Controlling, shoulders and arms, along with
Virgo, ruling the intestines.

Known as Wednesday, <u>Mercre</u>di,
Or the ruling planet: <u>Mercury</u>.
Or the consciousness of
Communication, intelligence and mental activity,
Male sexuality,
Mind, knowledge, thought, logic, reason,
Traveling, writing, speech, gossip and perceptions.

The number 3
Three thirds unified:
Body mind and soul.
A triangle.
Sky Blue, inspiration and communication.
How others see you:
Gracious, wise or stubborn and fierce like a raging bull.
Through use of your free will, and all you choose to do.

States of super consciousness
Determining the way you choose to personally self express.
The throat chakra of communication.
Words, voices, books, dictionary, **thesaurus**
Ruled by the star sign; Taurus.
Body part: wind pipe, throat, neck
Along with Libra ruling the kidneys.
Either side of your belly button
The divine reflection of how balance should be.

Also known to as Friday, Vendredi
Or the ruling planet: Venus.
Or the consciousness of Love, beauty, art and money
Harmony, inspiration, sociability,
Female sexuality,
Gratification, vanity, intimacy and rivalry

The number 4
The first whole or solid number.
North, east, south, west;
Spring, summer, autumn, winter,
Earth, air, fire, and water.

Pink (*white & red*) and **Green** (*Blue & yellow*).
Self healing and relationships,
Partners, marriages and friendships.

The plane of astral
Self determination, choice and will
Governs the planes of force and material

The Sub consciousness:
Your belief about love and relationships.

The heart chakra:
Ruled by the star sign Cancer.
Forgiveness and passion for others and self,
Emotional healing of negative, mental health.
Body parts: stomach, belly, breast, the colon and womb.
Known to us as <u>Mon</u>day, Lundi
Or ruling planet the moon.

The consciousness of:
Self acceptance and balanced compassion,
Instinct, memories, and emotions.
Down to earth, independent, complete foundations.
The mother;
Nurturing instinct, the past, reflection,
Receptivity, feelings, moods and emotional reactions.

The number 5
Man.
Awareness, adventure and freedom.
Senses, confidence.
Yellow: joy and wisdom.

Fire, the force plane
Of voluntary and involuntary actions,
Caused by your heart and mind's emotional reactions.

Consciousness of life
Heavenly blessed, or full of strife.
Self will and personal power
Will determine who you are.
Hidden in your spine and reflected to your chest
The chakra known as the solar plexus;
Determining which way your life shall go.
The Lion of Judah, ruled by the star sign Leo

5 if we count each toe and finger
Arm, leg, leg, arm, head: Allah
Should man stand in the shape of a 5 pointed star.

Self confidence and self esteem
Finding the courage to take risks, to be.
Life, will power, and creativity.
Body parts: heart, back and spine.
Fertile or sterility.

Known to us as <u>Sun</u>day, Dimanche
Or the ruling planet: the sun.
Or the consciousness of **Living life and having fun.**
Self identity, self expression, self integrity,
Recognition, potential, principle, vitality.
The father:
Consciousness, power and creativity

The number 6
Pregnant with love

Orange (Red & yellow): courage, energy,
Family,
Beauty and harmony;
Knowledge of who you are
Spiritually enslaved or divine, with all spiritual power.
What you do comes back to you;
You pay yourself back for the things that you do.

The chakra known as the sacral;
The consciousness which is interpersonal.
Body function: teeth, knees, and skeletal bones
All required before you are born.
Also known as the devil
Skull and bones, 666 or ruled by the
Horned star sign Capricorn.
Along with Aquarius
Ruling circulation, veins and shins.

Ruling planets Saturn and Uranus
Known to us as <u>Satur</u>day, Samedi
Or the consciousness of
Intuition, originality,
Structure and responsibility,
Discipline, boundaries, limitation.
Karma, fear, denial, resilience, and self condemnation,
Chaos, Change, higher mind, and invention.

The number 7
Spirituality.
Red: health and power.
The plane of material and physical,
The consciousness of the interpersonal
The plane of mental reflection
Reflected as earthly perception.

The base chakra: me, myself and I
Not just being alive
But standing up for one self, in order to survive.
Out of thousands of sperm, there's only one chosen one;
Once it travels down into the womb
The divine **all** is done.

Body function: the sexual organs;
Having the balls to dare.
Determine which of your insecurities basically go
Ruled by the star sign Scorpio,
Along with Aries ruling the muscles
And the ruling planet: Pluto
Known as the consciousness of
Destruction, transformation,
Rebirth and regeneration.
Power, abuse, pollution, and elimination.
The unconscious mind, compulsion and obsession

The number 8
Money.
Brown (orange & red), wealth and security,
Abundance, luck, and wisdom,

Philosophy and growth of exploration.
Body functions: the liver, the thighs, and the hips.
Ruled by the star sign Sagittarius.

Ruling planet: Jupiter,
Known to us as Thursday, <u>Jeu</u>di.
Or the consciousness of:
Hope, faith and philosophy,
Visualization, optimism, travel, wastage or generosity.

The number 9
Completion, invention growth,
Brown, your connection to the earth.
Last of the divine plan, your root to the ground,
Once became a chosen one
You were planted in the womb, nurtured in water like a fish.
Ruled by the star sign Pisces
Know as the consciousness,
Of The ability to reach goals and set targets,
Unable to focus, concentrate or lethargic.
Consciousness, awareness, listening,
Grounded, alert, and imagination.

38 Back 2 Reality – Mind over matter

To be grounded on earth a thought
Cannot work on its own;
It needs a body
In order for it to manifest creation physically.

'Its mind over matter.'
Only the more you know what you're actually doing
The stronger your energies are.

All the things we see:
Beauty, strange coincidence or spookey
Are all part of the natural functions of the human body.
The power of nature, the mind
And its creative capabilities.

Psychic, physician, physics, psychology
Psychiatric, psychiatrist, philosophy
Counsellors, therapists, martial artists, beauty
Art, music, dancing, drama and poetry

Matter and anti-matter
That which we can, and cannot, see.
The power of the divine reactions
Of positive and negativity
Manifested from the mind
Into the heart,
And throughout the body.

"Nutrition..."

Everything gets broken, stops working,
Falls apart or gets dirty;
Including the insides of our body.

Having a negative heart, a negative mind,
Or stressed out emotionally
Will takes its toll, and push its way
To the outside, eventually.

Dis–ease and illnesses
Cause blocked energies;
Therefore your body is unable to fight naturally.

Nutrition
Was made for us, naturally
To keep our body, mind and soul healthy.
Colourful
Fruits and vegetables,
Vitamins and minerals
Herbs and botanicals;
Such as peppermint, chamomile
Almond and witch hazel.
Hyssop, frankincense, irish moss
Ginger, sarsaparilla.
Apples, pears, strawberries, bananas,
Peas, cauliflower and cucumber
Iron, magnesium, zinc, potassium
Iodine, chorine and calcium

"Cleansing remedies, tonics and baths..."

Grandma's remedy was
To drink, wash with or rub onto your body.
Hubble bubble, boil and trouble
Make a quick magic fix on the double.
With the same ingredients we use in our soaps

Bubble baths or shampoos,
Deodorant, hair grease, skin and food.

She knew that
Naturally, infusing or boiling them is far more effective
Than manufactured products with mixed
Colourings, additives and preservatives.
These may look and smell better
But really, it's a choice between
Smelling nice, packaging and CANCER!

"Aromatherapy..."

With aromatherapy,
The sense of smell stimulates energy.
Scents such as orange, lemon grass, lavender,
Pine, sandalwood or rosemary,
Causing us to feel relaxed, calm
Alive, aroused or happy.

"Massage..."

Massage is a form
Of releasing chronic, muscular tension,
Reliving stress, improving lymph flow and blood circulation.

"Reflexology..."

Reflexology is a foot or hand massage,
Stimulating reflex points with direct links to the body,
Increasing the flow of energy.

"Crystals..."

Gems, birthstones and crystals
Are forms of minerals
Mainly used for jewellery,
With no knowledge that they heal;
Spiritually, mentally and physically.

Grown in the core of the earth in
The matrix bed,
Not just for fancy earrings, necklaces,
Rings and crowns for your head!
Black onyx, silvery pearl,
Pink rose quartz, selenite,
Gold, silver, red ruby, green emerald,
Tiger's eye and calcite.
Each one sending out a different
Colour-speed frequency
Vibration of energy.
Also used
As war head and missile ingredients,
Telescopes, X rays and some prescribed tablets.

"Affirmations..."

The computer is made on the principles
Of the body of a human.
The brain being the mother-board
And our thoughts and words the programmes.

'A... B ...C ...D ...E ...F ...G ...
H ...I ...J ...K ...L ...M ...N ...O ...P ...'
Programmed into us from nursery.
Words such as 'can't' are like a virus,

Programmed into your subconscious.
Those who are programmed to be late,
Will always be forced to change appointment dates;

They will never be on time,
No matter how hard their efforts may be,
They're programmed to sabotage the use of integrity;
Meaning what they actually say,
And doing it in exactly that way.

How you talk to yourself
Really makes a difference to you,
As well as everyone else.
'Each and every day I'm growing more and more'
Affirming positive thinking into your subconscious,
Stronger then before.

'I can, I will, get that far.'
' can, I will, cure this cancer.'
All is well;
With words, a magical *Spell*
Affirming a positive, past, present, and future.

"Psychic..."

Clairvoyants;
In tune to their gifts, naturally
And are able to recognise the vibration of
Thoughts and feelings of others' energy
Other than 'happy vibes' at a party,
Or thinking it's coincidently.

"Palm reading..."

The power in the Psalms
Is also in the palms.
Palm reading is a form of reading
The energies of the lines upon your hands
Which reflect your inner thoughts and feelings.

"Card readings..."

Each card displaying the general, basic ways of thinking of
Higher purpose, relationships, money,
Health, careers and family.

Wands: Fire; intuition, vision, progress, success, failure,
individuality.
Pentacles: Earth; sense of materialism
And external reality.
Swords: Air; thought, information, ideals
And self expression.
Cups: Water; feelings, relationships and emotion.
The cards, coincidently, apply to you
Because your sub conscious leads you to those cards.
They do not tell the future...you do!

Physically hearing what you want to hear
All of that of which you already know, but are unaware;
Your future is already there
It's there, waiting for you
And all depends on what you do,
Or do not, decide to do!

"In tune with nature..."

In order to receive a healing,
All you need to do is tune in
To nature, and your natural inner rhythm.
We do this when reciting
A nursery rhyme, a poem, a song or a hymn;
Through relaxation, meditation,
And self concentration;
Water, fresh air, and exercise.
Letting the tears fall from your eyes.
Not looking outwards, but by looking within,
And addressing and dealing with
Negative emotions and feelings.

39 Back 2 Reality – Fear

In order to foresee
The future; Spiritually, mentally or physically,
All we need to do is stop!
And think about certain things
And the reaction it will bring.

If you put a cup carelessly on the side,
There's a possibility that it may fall.
If you play football in the house,
There's a possibility you may break something
With the ball.

If you don't eat healthily,
There's a possibility you won't have a healthy body.
If you smoke,
It could possibly give you bad breath,
Cancer, or cause you to choke.
If you drink and drive,
You could endanger the possibility of someone else
Staying alive.
If you have sex without a condom,
There's a possibility, you'll have a daughter, or a son.

"Wisdom..."

Seeking mental wisdom
Creates a possibility of spiritual freedom.
We are like red and white blood cells in the earth
And, if we destroy ourselves, along with the earth,

There is no possibility that human beings
Will no longer have any worth.

If we all join in unity,
Despite our egos and insecurities,
No matter the description, or the name of God's identity,
There's a possibility we'd see life for how its supposed to be.
And I believe the one true 'God'" would be extremely happy!
...wouldn't S/He?

"Evolution"

For you to be thinking about your future
It means it's time to grow, and that you want something
better.
But by doing, or saying, nothing at all,
It's just as good as saying you like it, it's cool,
So,
You'll get your divine wish, again, and again, and again.
Because you want everything to stay the same.
You like to feel the pain! **You** like to pass the blame!
You are the captain of the illusion game,
And declaring your downfalls in the devil's name!

But through the pain you will see
One day, eventually
Dreams of living a heavenly life
Can only come true
If you manifest them here and now, physically,
By using the power of your positive capabilities.

"Eve-ill..."

Sending out,
Or taking on board, someone else's negativity,
As well as them, affects your life's possibilities.
If you use your physical, mental, or spiritual power

160

To cause intentional or unintentional destruction,
You too could end up dead, in prison,
In hospital, a mad house or on the run.
What you do comes back to you,
Because you made the thought, so what else should it do?

"Reality..."

If you keep ignoring your divine mission
There's a possibility you need to learn more lessons.
Lessons of life universally,
And opening your eyes to **REAL**ITY!
Travel through TIME, explore and learn
Life's possibilities:
Hover**crafts**, space**craft**, witch**craft**, or the human body.
Beauty, nature, arts and **crafts** or technology,
Or simply ghetto-bad-man mentality,
Or going by what you see on TV.,
Witch ever one it may be!
Learning to love the Divine, all unconditionally
Spiritually, emotionally and physically,
Acknowledging the power of your minds creativity.
Finding the confidence to let it be,
And then manifesting it on earth for all to see.
Making it more than hope, or a fairy tale,
A thought, or a just a dream.

"The All...!"

The power and ruling was given unto humans...
You and me,
The divine creation of positive and negativity,
We inherit from our Creator, 'Our creator,'.... you see.

So what you do, comes back to you
And your life affects my world too.
We **ALL** affect each other,

Everything, and everybody,
Because we're **ALL** interconnected, universally.
But, like children we go forth blindly, and ignorantly,
We prefer to make our own presumptions,
Instead of listening carefully.

"'Psssstt, you know I'm right,
I have been telling you from the start,'
So goes the silent whispering voice
Of your heart.

That whispering voice of
Knowledge of good and bad,
That whispering voice of
Knowledge of happiness and sad,
Not that which you learned from everyone else,
But that powerful knowledge of self

You see,
All the messages sent from above
Are all divine messages of the light, the truth, the way,
ONE LOVE.
And the root to love you will find
Is created by control
Over the power of your own mind.

40 Back 2 Reality – I found my identity

I acknowledge my divine mission, and now I see
I am the missing piece of the puzzle to discovering the real
me.
I've opened my mind to exploring
My possibilities and capabilities,
And the power of gaining control of my own mind's creativity.

Through strength and pride of my DNA herstory,
And true knowledge of my spirituality,
I acknowledge that what will be, will be.
Created by no external God,
Rather by part of the Most High Creator,
Inside of you, me and everybody.

Now my eyes are open, I clearly see
All that I believe
Is all that I achieve.
I can be anything I want to be.
I control my destiny
And each and every possibility.
I opened my eyes and now I am aware
What's done in Heaven, will be done on Earth;
So we won't be going anywhere!

They say the meek will inherit the earth,
I believe if there were no bottom
The top wouldn't have any worth.
I ac**know**ledge, I have a choice to choose either one
And once I do that, it's signed sealed and done.

"I know because"...

I ac**know**ledge the Most High Creator,
And the power and responsibility
That was given unto me.
I ac**know**ledge that I was made in image of my creator
And just like Him/Her,
On the inside and out there's only one me!

I ac**know**ledge my leadership and mothering skills
In my masculine and feminine sexuality.
I ac**know**ledge the power of my minds creativity.
I ac**know**ledge my trials and tribulations
Derived from my positive and negative qualities.
I ac**know**ledge there are always two sides to a story
And each one of these can always be told in its own glory
I ac**know**ledge all the things I hide inside
Which cause insecurities to affect my pride.

I ac**know**ledge the divine balance of wrong and right
I believe in myself and not what I see with my eyesight.
I ac**know**ledge why it's wrong to judge others personalities
Which are made from their unique perceptions and not my
mentality. I ac**know**ledge the divine lesson of learning
How to love like a God - Unconditionally!

I ac**know**ledge that for each and every action
I pay myself back with a reaction;
Whether that be Love,
Happiness, or total destruction.

I ac**know**ledge my divine all-responsibility
To my planet, myself, my family, and my community;
With love, respect and unity,
Along with the financial aspects of security.

Now that I have found myself
The advice I bring to you
My Brother, and my sister, is
Get to know yourself well too!

Lightning Source UK Ltd.
Milton Keynes UK
UKOW020307300911

179494UK00001B/3/P